People will make time for things that are most important to them. Although God is not a thing for us to fit into our schedules, we do have to prioritize time to engage with Him. Kerry combines her theological insights with life experiences and gives us a book—actually, a ready-made process—to help us deepen our engagement with God.

Try it: turn aside from your busyness, give God your attention through this book, and watch how your intimacy with Him will begin to grow.

—DOUG CLAY
General Superintendent of the Assemblies of God, USA

Nothing is more important than connecting with God Himself. We should serve Him up close and personal, not from afar. Even though this is the one relationship above all others that we must continually strengthen and deepen, many people find this to be challenging and keep circling back. Kerry Clarensau is an articulate author as well as being insightful, practical, and spiritually astute. You won't want to miss *Engaging with God* because she selected some fresh approaches and takes us on an eight-week journey accompanied by Bible, prayer, and journaling. Better habits and a closer connection with the Lord are bound to result.

—CAROLYN TENNANT, PhD.
Speaker, author,
Vice President Emerita at North Central University (Minneapolis), and
faculty in the D.Min. Program at AGTS (Springfield, Missouri)

Since the beginning, God has desired an intimate relationship with His children. In fact, it is personified with God walking in the cool of the day with Adam and Eve and later through the life of Jesus as He walked and lived among us as part of God's redemptive plan. In her book, Kerry Clarensau invites us to take a walk with Jesus marked by intentional intimacy and the stillness of our soul.

Her personal stories will encourage you. The way she illustrates the truths of God's Word will enliven you. And her daily prompts are sure to engage you into a richer and closer walk with Jesus.

—DR. MELISSA J. ALFARO
Executive Presbyter Representing Under-40 Ministers for the General
Council of the Assemblies of God, USA; a pastor of El Tabernaculo
Assembly of God in Houston, Texas; communicator, writer, blogger

When you read Kerry Clarensau's new book, *Engaging with God*, you will become anxious to clear your mind of the clutter, rearrange your busy schedule, and find your "secret place" so you can deepen your relationship with the Creator who desires to fellowship with His creation. Allow Kerry to guide you on a spiritual journey by providing meaningful devotions with detailed prayer prompts designed to eliminate any questions about how to consistently engage with God. This book will not be one you read only once. It will become a lifelong companion, a treasured resource in your personal growth plan.

—ALTON GARRISON
Acts 2 Journey Executive Director
Former Assistant General Superintendent, Assemblies of God, USA

Having a sustaining relationship with God involves a two-way conversation. Most of us know how to ask God on behalf of our needs or wants, but we may not understand how God speaks to us. *Engaging with God* offers eight ways to develo a deep friendship with God where we are captivated and mentored in His response. This is a book that will hearten your time with God.

—COLEEN SCHABERG
Wyoming Network WYSOM director

Sometimes you see the words "life-changing" and it's easy to gloss over them as being an exaggeration. *Engaging with God: Eight Life-Changing Practices to Experience All He Has for You* is not a book you simply gloss over. This book is written from the heart of a woman who has saturated herself in God's Word, and we get the benefit of that time on these pages. Kerry has taken Scriptures and made them easily understandable and digestible. If we follow the prompts and take her wisdom to heart it is truly *life-changing*. Thank you, Kerry, for opening the door and allowing us, the readers, to infiltrate the intimacy you have with Jesus and show us how we can do exactly the same.

—SHEILA HARPER
Founder and President, SaveOne

Kerry has done it again! She has once again called us to rise above our works and back into a deep and fulfilling relationship with God. Back to hearing, knowing, and experiencing Him, not just serving. This writing is both a motivational appetizer that makes you want to know, taste, and experience God, and a clear path to the table. Good job, Kerry!

—RICK DUBOSE
Assistant General Superintendent of the Assemblies of God, USA

Engaging with God: Eight Life-Changing Practices to Experience All He Has for You is a must-read for any believer seeking to abide in God's presence. Kerry's honest and open appeal to her readers encourages intentionality in practicing the disciplines of engaging with God. She shares enlightening, challenging, and simple applications transformative to the Christian journey. The truths she relates are practical and meaningful in their influence and they encourage a humble, listening approach to our relationship with God. Applying the principles she relays deepened my relationship with the Lord.

—MICHELLE PARKS, EdD
Credentialed minister, pastor's wife, teacher

Engaging with God is an experience worth the investment. To Kerry this is a way of life and not only a great idea worthy to be shared. The anointing of God is so evident and powerful in Kerry's life. I have had the honor of seeing Kerry live out the topics written in this devotional to bless you and me. And I have been immensely blessed by my own encounters with God under the careful guidance of Kerry's powerful words in this devotional. I can't imagine living the rest of my life without the specific element of engaging God on a regular basis.

My hope and prayer is that you will also be blessed by Kerry's life-giving, life-changing, and life-transforming words. Read and work through this devotional with great expectation. God is ready to be engaged, and Kerry will help guide you through the process. I trust that you will experience God transformation after every God encounter.

—ADRIANA LUNGU
Missionary and Co-Founder of Chi Alpha Moldova and Genesis Church, Moldova

In James 4:8, we find the most incredible invitation and promise ever delivered, "Come near to God, and He will come near to you." Yes, the Creator of the Universe and of all humanity desires to have a close relationship and fellowship with us. Indeed, as we learn to walk more closely with God, our love for Him and His will for our lives will grow and continue to change us in amazing ways.

There are benefits and rewards for those who walk closely with God. In Kerry Clarensau's new book, *Engaging with God,* she unpacks this truth and provides eight life-changing practices that will help us dive deeper into our relationship with God. As you learn and engage these practices, anticipate being inspired, challenged, and encouraged by Kerry's biblical insights and personal experiences. Are you ready to respond to God's invitation?

—JOSHUA AND LAVAN RIVERA
Founding Pastors, Fuego Church

Engaging with God is a treasure trove of encouragement and instruction to help lead you into an intimate relationship with God and keep you on that path for life. Within these pages you will not only find biblical examples but also practical guidelines for cultivating a vibrant walk with God, hearing His voice, and living a life aligned with Scripture. Destined to be a classic, *Engaging with God* merits a place with the books you turn to again and again.

—KAY BURNETT
Author, former National Director of Women's Ministries for the Assemblies of God, USA

Are you looking for a book to guide you deeper in your life and leadership? *Engaging with God* captures life-giving practices that lead to life-changing ways. Through her brilliant writing, using story and study, Kerry has designed an eight-week journey to take you into the deep "with God" to experience God.

—LISA POTTER
Author, *The Collective Journey: An Invitation to Go Deeper in Your Life and Leadership*
Executive Director, Women Who Lead and Roar

Communication is key in any relationship, and certainly a key element for a passionate, maturing relationship with Jesus. However, fostering an intimate connection with the Creator of the Universe can sound daunting! What does that look like in a practical way?

I'm so thankful Kerry has beautifully charted a course to not just know about God but to encounter His presence. *Engaging with God* is an eight-week pathway that will deepen your understanding, guide you in prayer, and tune your ear to the Master's voice. May God use the tool that is in your hand to fan the flame of your heart to know Him more.

—NONDA HOUSTON
National Director of Women's Ministries for the Assemblies of God, USA

Scripture quotations marked NIV are taken from the Holy Bible, New International Version®, NIV®. Copyright © 1973, 1978, 1984, 2011 by Biblica, Inc.™ Used by permission of Zondervan. All rights reserved worldwide. www.zondervan.com. The "NIV" and "New International Version" are trademarks registered in the United States Patent and Trademark Office by Biblica, Inc.™ | Scripture quotations marked NLT are taken from the Holy Bible, New Living Translation, copyright © 1996, 2004, 2015 by Tyndale House Foundation. Used by permission of Tyndale House Publishers, Inc., Carol Stream, Illinois 60188. All rights reserved. | The ESV® Bible (The Holy Bible, English Standard Version®). ESV® Text Edition: 2016. Copyright © 2001 by Crossway, a publishing ministry of Good News Publishers. The ESV® text has been reproduced in cooperation with and by permission of Good News Publishers. Unauthorized reproduction of this publication is prohibited. All rights reserved. | All Scripture quotations marked TPT are from The Passion Translation®. Copyright © 2017, 2018, 2020 by Passion & Fire Ministries, Inc. Used by permission. All rights reserved. ThePassionTranslation.com.

For foreign and subsidiary rights, contact the author.

Cover design by Sara Young

ISBN: 978-1-957369-28-0   1 2 3 4 5 6 7 8 9 10

Printed in the United States of America

KERRY CLARENSAU

Engaging with GOD

EIGHT LIFE-CHANGING PRACTICES TO EXPERIENCE ALL HE HAS FOR YOU

ARROWS & STONES

OTHER BOOKS BY KERRY CLARENSAU

Secrets: Transforming Your Life and Marriage
Springfield, MO: Gospel Publishing House, 2009.

Love Revealed: Experiencing God's Authentic Love,
Springfield, MO: Influence Resources, 2011.

Redeemed: Embracing a Transformed Life,
Springfield, MO: My Healthy Church, 2012.

A Beautiful Life:Discovering the Freedom of Selfless Love,
Springfield, MO: Influence Resources, 2014.

Fully His: Make the Life God Offers Your Own,
Springfield, MO: Gospel Publishing Houses, 2016.

Adored: by The God Who Sees Me,
Springfield, MO: Gospel Publishing House, 2018.

DEDICATION

This book is dedicated to my mentor, Peggy Musgrove. I find it challenging to describe her in a few words. She was a woman of integrity and faithfulness. She was confident, yet humble. Peggy was a gifted communicator, leader, and teacher of the Word. Looking back, I see how God strategically placed her in my life when I was only 25 years old. The first time we met we had no idea how integrated our journeys would become. Peggy and her husband were lead pastors of a congregation in Wichita, Kansas where my husband and I would later serve. We also worked together on a daily basis in two different settings, spanning more than a decade. And each of us served as the national women's director for our denomination. She was a constant guide to me as I worked in the local church and national office. Even though Peggy passed away in 2020, her example continues to inspire me, and I will always be grateful for her investment in my life. God used Peggy to help prepare me for the various positions I would fill, but along the way she gave me something worth so much more—she taught me the value of engaging with God.

ACKNOWLEDGEMENTS

First of all, I want to thank Dr. Carolyn Tennant for the insights she shared in a seminary course on spiritual formation. The time in her classroom ignited an overwhelming desire in me to engage with God. The practices she taught in the classroom worked their way into my daily life and were a catalyst for this book. I am forever grateful.

I also want to thank Kay Burnett, Sherri Campbell, Adriana Lungu, and Lisa Pettitt for allowing me to talk through my early thoughts on this project. I am an out-loud processor and their time was an invaluable gift.

Michelle Parks and Coleen Schaberg gave huge amounts of time to read the material as I was developing it. Their insights made this project so much better. "Thank you" doesn't seem adequate for their investment.

I want to express my gratitude to the amazing team at Four Rivers Publishing for their willingness to take these words and make them in to what you hold in your hands today.

Our son, Tyler, edited and gave a much-needed perspective to this work. His commitment to the integrity of the Word inspires me! I'm really proud to be his mom.

And finally, I want to thank the greatest contributor to my writing—my amazing husband, Mike. He has cheered me on, provided theological insights, proofed copy, brainstormed titles and thoughts, and made his own meals and eaten alone when I was in the writing zone. I couldn't have done it without his help and support. He's just the greatest!

Contents

ENGAGING WITH GOD

INTRODUCTION

Friends and acquaintances—two completely different types of relationships. When I think of my closest friends, I think about those people I talk with on a regular basis. Our times together are often marked by meaningful, deep conversations. (And sometimes we just talk about the crazy weather or our dinner plans.) My friend shares and then I share. We listen and respond to what each other says. Over time, the relationship grows and we learn how to encourage and inspire good things in each other. These friendships are life-giving as a result of quality, ongoing communication.

On the other hand, acquaintances are individuals we may know from work or the neighborhood, and we simply haven't had the opportunity to build a friendship with them. Most of us have many acquaintances in our lives—people who we know, but not well enough to call a friend. Others are acquaintances for a completely different reason. We may encounter them frequently enough to become friends, but the interactions we have with them hinder the development of the relationship. When we are together, the communication is mostly one-sided. The acquaintances talk and talk, without hardly taking a breath. They don't allow time for feedback or response. Since they are *consumed by what is on their heart*, they hardly notice the other person at all. We can walk away from that type of an encounter and wonder if the person even knew we were there. Quality relationships cannot be built with these types of interactions.

> I propose that hearing from God and growing in our knowledge of Him is the most important part of our encounters with Him.

The same idea comes into play in our relationship with God. Many times we can interact with God like the individuals I referred to as "acquaintances." We are so consumed with what is on our mind that we simply rush into our devotional time, read a few passages of Scripture, and then pour out our many requests. When we fail to quiet our own hearts enough to turn our attention to Who He is and what He might want to say to us, we miss so much.

I propose that hearing from God and growing in our knowledge of Him is the most important part of our encounters with Him. After all, our side of the conversation is rather limited. Just think about it:

» He is the Creator and sustainer of life—we are the created and completely dependent upon Him
» He is all-knowing—we are limited by our experience and education
» He is faithful and unchanging—we are ever so fickle
» He is loving and kind—we tend to be self-absorbed
» He is redemptive and focused on eternity—we can be fixated on our current circumstances

As we deeply consider His character, we understand how engaging with Him could bring incredible fulfillment to our lives. God speaking to us *and* us responding to what He has to say.

Hearing from God may seem like it is just for a select few. But it is not! He wants to speak with you, I promise! Just imagine receiving His wisdom for the challenges you are facing today. Or what about gaining His eternal perspective on the decision you need to make this week? Think about the peace we can experience as we learn to rest in His steadfast love. Doesn't it feel a bit tragic if we sit down with our Creator God and we are the ones doing all the talking?

While we know He is ever-present, we need to understand how to engage in two-way communication with a God who rarely speaks audibly. When we anticipate hearing from God, He speaks to us in a variety of ways. Sometimes He gets our attention through His creation. A brilliant sunrise can remind us of His faithfulness and how His mercies are new every morning. God can speak to us through a friend or a pastor as they talk about His Truth. He can get our attention through the innocent words of a child or through the lyrics of a song that "randomly" comes to our minds. However, the number one way He speaks to us is through His written Word.

Engaging with God is so much more than simply reading a few verses and making our requests known to God. A close relationship with God involves these eight practices:

» **Turning** into His presence
» **Remembering** who He is and all He does
» **Listening** diligently to His Word
» **Responding** to His voice
» **Asking** for His involvement
» **Waiting** for His response
» **Wrestling** with His will
» **Anticipating** His goodness

To be transparent, these ideas have taken me decades to understand and implement. While I still have so much to learn, I continually discover He has so much for us to experience as we faithfully engage with Him. No matter where you are on your spiritual journey, may this devotional/prayer guide deepen your relationship with your Redeemer and help you experience all He has for you.

Paul's prayer for the believers in Colossae has become my prayer for you as you walk through this eight-week journey . . .

"(I) ask God to give you complete knowledge of his will and to give you spiritual wisdom and understanding. Then the way you live will always honor and please the Lord, and your lives will produce every kind of good fruit. All the while, you will grow as you learn to know God better and better. We also pray that you will be strengthened with all his glorious power so you will have all the endurance and patience you need. May you be filled with joy, always thanking the Father. He has enabled you to share in the inheritance that belongs to his people, who live in the light. For he has rescued us from the kingdom of darkness and transferred us into the Kingdom of his dear Son, who purchased our freedom and forgave our sins."

–Colossians 1:9-14 (NLT)

HOW TO USE THIS DEVOTIONAL/PRAYER GUIDE

1) This devotional is divided into eight weekly sessions and is designed to assist you in engaging with God. Each week begins by looking at particular portions of Scripture and a few thoughts from the passages regarding the topic for that session. Read through Scripture passages and those pages before engaging in the *Daily Prayer Prompts*.

2) Consider reading the verses in several translations of the Bible—this can help you to understand the passages more clearly. God's Word is the key component of this journey. What I share is simply a guide to help you engage with Him and His Word.

3) The five *Daily Prayer Prompts* are designed to help you go deeper into the truths of Scripture as you process them in His presence. Ask the Lord what He would like for you to remember from the passages you read. Listen closely and respond to what you hear Him say in His Word. Write out your thoughts—this is a great way to process and communicate with God. It is also a way to go back and remember those things He speaks to your heart.

4) At the end of each week, respond to the "End-of-the-Week Journal Prompts" to further solidify what God is speaking to you. You might want to meet with a friend or a small group of friends who are also walking through this devotional. Use the "End-of-the-Week Journal Prompts" to get the conversation started. Each person will bring a unique perspective and you can learn so much from one another.

5) Small Group Weekly Guides are located in the back of this book to assist you if you are taking this journey within your community of friends.

GUIDE FOR A DAY ALONE WITH GOD

Several years ago, I took a seminary class which required me to spend 24 hours alone with God. To be completely honest with you, it was a bit intimidating—*what would I do for an entire day*? Well, I jumped in and discovered there was nothing quite like spending extended time alone with God. It was an amazing experience. And I want you to experience it too. Since it can be intimidating, I've developed a guide to help you engage with God throughout the course of several hours. This guide is found at the back of this devotional. Even if you can't take a full day, plan to spend as many hours as you can engaging with God. I realize it will take some effort to make this happen, but it will be worth it. I promise!

TURNING INTO HIS PRESENCE

WEEK ONE
TURNING

**EXODUS 3:1-6, MATTHEW 6:6, LUKE 10:38-42,
NEHEMIAH 1-2:8, PSALM 119:37**

Mike and I love those evenings when we can relax on the sofa together at the end of a busy day. It's a time for us to connect with each other before calling it a night. Since we've spent quite a few years together, I can't remember all of them in detail, but I do remember one evening with great clarity. We sat on each side of our son, Tyler, who was around four years old at the time. It had been a difficult day for all of us. Our youngest son, Blake, was just a few months old and he wasn't sleeping well and demanded a lot of extra attention. When Blake fell asleep that night, Tyler was excited to have us all to himself. However, I was exhausted from taking care of a fussy infant and wanted to sit quietly and zone out. (Every parent of little ones can relate!)

While Mike and I watched television, Tyler talked non-stop. I heard him, but I was too tired to focus on what he was saying. I simply gave the occasional, "Umm, really?" Tyler knew I wasn't listening, so he decided to do something about it. He got up on his knees and leaned against my side. I can still feel his little hands on each side of my face as he turned my head to face him. He looked deeply into my eyes, and said, "Mommy, really listen to me." He gently held on to my cheeks as he poured out his thoughts. While I don't remember what he said, I do remember how he made me feel. I was heartbroken because he wanted to interact with me and I was too tired and distracted to give him the attention he craved. Poor little guy! Tyler knew I needed to turn and face him, or he wouldn't be heard.

Life is full of things that keep our hearts and minds occupied—even distracted. I wonder how many times the Lord might want to "take our face" in "His hands" and turn our focus to Him.

> Life is full of things that keep our hearts and minds occupied—even distracted. I wonder how many times the Lord might want to "take our face" in "His hands" and turn our focus to Him.

For those of us who have chosen to follow Jesus, we know God is always with us, and throughout Scripture we see how God is near. Yet, in those same passages we read how we have to intentionally turn our attention from what is going on around us to focus fully on Him. When we turn and give Him our undivided attention, we begin to experience His presence and activity in a whole new way because we are fully engaged with Him.

Let's take a look at a few portions of Scripture to help us understand this idea. While these passages differ greatly from one another, each one helps us to understand the practice of "turning" more clearly.

#1 Exodus 3:1-6

In Exodus 3, we read the story of Moses and the burning bush: "Now Moses was keeping the flock of his father-in-law, Jethro, the priest of Midian, and he led his flock to the west side of the wilderness and came to Horeb, the mountain of God. And the angel of the Lord appeared to him in a flame of fire out of the midst of a bush. He looked, and behold, the bush was burning, yet it was not consumed. And Moses said, I will turn aside to see this great sight, why the bush is not burned. **When the Lord saw that he turned aside to see, God called to him out of the bush**, 'Moses, Moses!' And he said, 'Here I am,'" Exodus 3:1-4.

Ruth Haley Barton says, "There seems to be a cause and effect relationship between Moses' willingness to pay attention and God's willingness to speak . . . God spoke because Moses stopped, paused, noticed and turned aside!"[1]

How intriguing! Could we miss hearing the voice of God because we don't notice His activity and take the time to stop what we are doing and turn toward Him? His activity is all around us, yet most of the time we simply walk right past Him because we are too busy to notice. I pray we become more like Moses and take the time to stop, notice, and turn aside. God wants us to know Him, hear His voice, and join Him in His activity by turning to Him. Exodus 3 and 4 show us the types of conversations God wants to have with His children when they turn aside to listen.

1   Strengthening the Soul of Your Leadership, page 61

#2 Matthew 6:6

Jesus gave us a lot of simple, yet impactful instructions. When it comes to this idea of turning and engaging with our Heavenly Father, He knows how easily we are distracted. So He provided clear directions in Matthew 6:6: "But when you pray, **go into your room and shut the door and pray to your Father who is in secret**." Jesus was warning His disciples about praying to be seen by others. However, Jesus is also telling us about the importance of meeting with God alone. As we turn aside from other relationships and close ourselves away with God, we can focus on Him by listening intently to His Word and responding to what He says. It is there, in that secret place—away from distractions, where we can hear His voice and then humbly and completely make ourselves known to Him.

Notice what Jesus says about *how* God responds when we "go into our room, close the door and pray." He says, "And your Father who sees in secret will **reward** you." The writer of Hebrews tells us that God rewards those who seek him (Hebrews 11:6). I've discovered those rewards to be invaluable! In those quiet moments, God reveals His will, His character, His presence, and His purposes in a deep way. Growing more aware of Who He is increases my faith and gives me such hope. My focus shifts from all that is going on around me onto His goodness and love. This changes me by adjusting my attitudes and realigning my expectations. My time alone with God is the best part of the day!

> Our souls desperately need those times when we turn aside from others and give Him our full attention.

I rarely miss it because the rewards are so sweet. Our souls desperately need those times when we turn aside from others and give Him our full attention.

#3 Luke 10:38-42

We gain additional insights about turning from distractions in Luke 10:38-42. Jesus and His disciples visit the home of two sisters, Martha and Mary. Each sister was there *with* Jesus, yet they engaged with Him quite differently from one another. Let's look closely at this story with our focus on what we learn from Jesus's interactions with them.

Mary chose to sit and listen to Jesus's teaching, but Martha was distracted by all of the preparations (Luke 10:40, NIV). She was frustrated with Mary's "inactivity" and desperately wanted her help. Martha interrupted Jesus's teaching to point out what she thought was Mary's idleness, and she asked Him to tell her sister to get busy. We could talk about Martha's apparent temperament or the interesting family dynamics, but let's just consider Jesus's response, "Martha, Martha, you are worried and upset about many things, but few things are needed—or indeed only one. Mary has chosen what is better, and it will not be taken from her," (Luke 10:41-42, NIV).

We know Martha wasn't just distracted with the preparations of serving, because Jesus points out how she was troubled about *many* things (verse 41). He has a way of looking below the surface and seeing the situation for all it is. Jesus told her that worry isn't necessary, but she did need **one thing**. It was the thing Mary chose—to sit in His presence and listen to His teaching. Jesus knew her real need wasn't Mary's help. Martha needed something she would discover when she gave Jesus her full attention.

I'm blown away at those words of Jesus, "one thing is needed." *One thing? Really? Just one thing?* Yes, my friend! One thing! He wants us to engage with Him by turning into His presence and pressing into what He says. This changes everything. Fear subsides, perspective is renewed, strength is gained, wisdom is found, peace engulfs us, love floods our hearts, joy rises above circumstances, hope floods in, and trust becomes our foundation. All of these rewards are available when we turn aside from the distractions and look full in His face.

#4 Nehemiah 1-2:8

The book of Nehemiah begins with the prophet hearing how the Israelites were in trouble because the wall of Jerusalem was broken down and the gates were destroyed by fire. Nehemiah responded by immediately turning to God with all of his heart, soul, and mind. He wept, fasted, and prayed. This is a great response to difficulty! But what I want you to notice today is found in chapter 2, verse 4, "Then the king said to me, 'What are you requesting?' So I prayed to the God of heaven. And I said to the king . . . " Even while Nehemiah was talking with the king, his heart turned toward the Lord in prayer.

While we desperately need time to pull away from everything and turn our full attention toward the Lord, we eventually have to leave those quiet places and step into our responsibilities. Nehemiah shows us how to turn our hearts toward Him as we fulfill our obligations and interact with those around us. We can so posture ourselves that even while we are working, our hearts continually turn to Jesus.

Each year I read a short book entitled *"The Practice of the Presence of God"* by Brother Lawerence. This man's goal was to turn his attention to the presence of God in the routine moments of life. Every time I read it, I'm reminded how we can turn in to His presence no matter what is going on around us. Whether we are talking with kings or wiping runny noses, God is near and able to guide us if we just turn our hearts and minds to engage with Him.

#5 Psalm 119:37

Psalm 119 is the longest chapter in the Bible and it focuses on the value of experiencing God's Word. In this prayer, the psalmist proclaims the benefits of living according to Scripture and he asks God to expand his understanding of the Word to experience even more of those rewards.

Verse 37 is a perfect prayer for us (well, at least it is one I need to pray every day): "Turn my eyes from looking at worthless things: and give me life in your ways."

It is so easy for us to spend hours on worthless things—scrolling through social media, watching YouTube videos, or allowing one of those pop-up ads to take 30 minutes of our precious time. With the amount of information available to us, the list of time-stealers is endless. Apart from wasting time on those things we find on our devices, we can take rabbit trails with our work, spend time worrying about a situation, or strive to achieve something which amounts to very little.

Some things may not be truly *worthless*, but they are *worth less* than our pursuit of God. We may feel that we don't have time or energy to engage with God in a meaningful way. And it is true, many seasons of life are chocked full of round-the-clock responsibilities (like working outside the home while parenting a small child, or caring for an aging parent or sick spouse). No matter what our responsibilities look like at the moment, we need to continually examine where we are spending time on things that are *worth less* than the **one thing** Jesus mentioned to Martha.

> Some things may not be truly worthless, but they are worth less than our pursuit of God.

In each of these biblical examples, the individuals had to turn aside from their daily responsibilities or distractions to experience what God had for them. Moses was doing his job, Martha and Mary were hosting and serving, Nehemiah was taking care of a national crisis, and the psalmist was tempted to spend time on worthless things. Even Jesus challenged His disciples (and us) to pull away from others to pray to our Father in secret.

We desperately need to think about what it looks like for us to turn aside and give God our full attention. For the next five days, study, meditate, and engage with these portions of Scripture. Take time to turn away from things that are *worth less* and pay attention to what the Lord wants you to know from each passage. I've provided some thoughts to nudge you as you turn. Use the space provided to process your thoughts in writing or to record what you hear the Lord speaking to you.

DAY 1
PRAYER PROMPT

READ EXODUS 3

God is so very near. His creation surrounds us. His written Word is readily available to us. God speaks to us through our pastors and our community of believers. He uses our situations and circumstances to teach us and lead us on the path He has for us. However, we can be too busy or distracted to recognize His activity. Take some time today to turn and notice. I'm not sure what this will look like for you, but here are some ideas and questions to get you started:

» Deeply consider the sermon you heard on Sunday.
» Consider passages of Scripture you most recently read. What do you learn about God in those verses?
» Where do you feel His presence the most?
» What activities or situations give you life?
» Which activities drain you?
» What is heavy on your heart?
» Is God trying to get your attention through a circumstance in your life?

Take some time to turn toward Him and listen for what He wants to say to you concerning those things.

DAY 2
PRAYER PROMPT

READ MATTHEW 6:6

How are you doing at following Jesus's instructions to "go into your room and shut the door and pray to your Father who is in secret?" If you faithfully turn aside from all other relationships to shut yourself in with God, thank Him for the opportunities you have to meet alone with Him. Consider deeply what these words of Jesus mean for you, "And your Father who sees in secret will reward you." Write out some of the "rewards" you have experienced. If you are not in the habit of pulling away and spending time alone with Him, ask Him to help you to make this a priority. Take 15 minutes today to be alone with God. Make a fresh commitment to spend time alone with God every day this week, and look for the rewards as you put this discipline into practice.

_____

_____

_____

_____

_____

_____

_____

_____

_____

_____

_____

_____

_____

_____

_____

DAY 3
PRAYER PROMPT

READ LUKE 10:38-42

Read Jesus's words to Martha several times. He says, "Martha, Martha, you are anxious and troubled about many things, but one thing is necessary. Mary has chosen the good portion, which will not be taken from her," Luke 10:41-42. Ask the Lord to show you if you are anxious and troubled. Ask Him to help you to understand what He means when He says, "One thing is necessary." Look back at verse 39 and consider what Mary had chosen. How can you give greater attention to the "one thing"? What are distractions for you? List those out, and give those things that are *worth less* to the Lord. Ask Him to help you choose the "one thing."

_____

_____

_____

_____

_____

_____

_____

_____

_____

_____

_____

_____

_____

_____

_____

_____

_____

_____

DAY 4
PRAYER PROMPT

READ NEHEMIAH 1-2:8

After Nehemiah takes the time to weep, pray and fast, he gets up and engages in his responsibilities. However, even when he is going about his work, he takes time to turn his heart towards the Lord in prayer. Think about the day ahead of you:

» What would it look like for you to turn toward His presence as you work through a difficult situation at work today?
» How can you turn to Him when you interact with your family or neighbors?
» Pray through the responsibilities in front of you and ask the Lord to remind you to turn to Him for help with each one.

_____

_____

_____

_____

_____

_____

_____

_____

_____

_____

_____

_____

_____

_____

_____

_____

DAY 5
PRAYER PROMPT

READ PSALM 119:37

The psalmist asks the Lord, "Turn my eyes from looking at worthless things; give me life in your ways."

Pray this verse. Allow the Lord to point out those things occupying your time that are worth less than pursuing Him. Write out your commitment to turn away from them. Then read as much of Psalm 119 as time allows. Highlight or write out the blessings of turning your attention to God's Word. How have you seen these rewards or blessings in your life? What do you think would be different about your life/day/relationships if you spent more time in the Word?

_____

_____

_____

_____

_____

_____

_____

_____

_____

_____

_____

_____

_____

_____

_____

END-OF-THE-WEEK JOURNAL PROMPTS

1) Which verse from this week's devotions impacted you the most and why?

_____

_____

_____

_____

_____

2) Describe a time in your life when God wanted to get your attention and you were too distracted to notice? What do you think would be different now if you had paid attention?

_____

_____

_____

_____

_____

3) How does it make you feel to know that God wants you turn aside from other relationships and spend time alone with Him?

_____

_____

_____

_____

_____

4) If you are in the practice of spending time alone with God every day, describe the "rewards" you have experienced.

_____

_____

_____

_____

_____

_____

5) Where are you tempted to be so busy serving that you forget to be with the One who called you to serve?

_____

_____

_____

_____

_____

6) What does it look like for you to purposefully turn your heart and mind toward Jesus as you are fulfilling your daily responsibilities?

_____

_____

_____

_____

_____

7) Did you identify anything worth less currently occupying your time? How do you discipline yourself to turn away from things that are worth less than your pursuit of God?

_____

_____

_____

_____

_____

REMEMBERING WHO HE IS AND ALL HE DOES

WEEK TWO

REMEMBERING

PSALM 145

What's going on in your world at this moment in time? Most likely you have family and friends to care for, work to be done, bills to pay, and belongings to maintain or repair. Your physical body requires nourishment and exercise on the good days, and extra care when you are fighting an illness. Each of your responsibilities creates multiple opportunities for problem solving. Let's be honest, even when life is sweet, we face challenges. Jesus said it this way, "Each day has enough trouble of its own" (Matthew 6:34, NIV).

I don't know about you, but I'm easily consumed by all of the situations surrounding my life. My thoughts are often focused on the tasks I need to accomplish or the situations I wish were different. I find myself giving little or no thought at all to how God is working and involved in my life. I realize this is a situation-bound way to live! I like to call this condition, "abiding in my circumstances." It is embarrassing to admit how often I find myself dwelling right there, in the middle of all my "stuff!" Maybe, I'm not alone in this. *Could it be a human tendency to focus on what is going on right around us and essentially ignore the One who created us and loves us extravagantly?*

When we find ourselves "abiding in our circumstances," our prayers are typically a list of problems—one right after the other. Then, we tell God how He should step in and make things right. (After all, we know what is best, right?) When we focus solely on all the situations we wish were different, we tend to overlook *who* we are actually talking with and we miss so much. Unfortunately, I'm speaking from experience. I have prayed this way far too many times to count. However, God offers us so much more in prayer than simply an opportunity to focus on the challenges of life!

If we want to experience His presence and activity, we have to be intentional about taking our eyes off of ourselves and all of the things swirling around in our hearts. I've discovered the best way to shift our focus is to **remember**. We can remind ourselves of who He is and all of the ways He blesses our lives. Even in the most challenging seasons, God is still good and His goodness surrounds us every day.

> Could it be a human tendency to focus on what is going on right around us and essentially ignore the One who created us and loves us extravagantly?

The Hebrew word for gratitude literally translated is "recognizing the good." When we make the effort to notice the good things, we are actually acknowledging God's activity in our lives. Scripture tells us to enter His presence with praise and thanksgiving. We should come to Him with a grateful heart. This can only happen as we train ourselves to see His blessings, especially the small, seemingly insignificant things—like a gentle rain shower, a good night's rest, or a warm meal. Recognizing His goodness has a way of calming our hearts and giving us incredible hope. It changes the way we see our circumstances and strengthens our faith. Gratitude also keeps us humble and in a right relationship with God because we acknowledge He is our Source and Sustainer.

Because we tend to be so forgetful, we must intentionally *remember*. Reading the Psalms and other parts of Scripture reminds us of who He is and how He provides for His children. We can also keep a gratitude journal to turn our thoughts to the good things He has done. Both of these activities (reading and journaling) help to increase our faith. They prompt different kinds of prayers than when we are simply focused on all of the things we wish were different. So friends, once we have turned into His presence, we need to be very intentional about remembering who He is and all of the good things He has done for us.

Take some time to read Psalm 145 and then read the paragraphs below which highlight the way David remembered God as he prayed.

#1 Psalm 145:1-3

"Every day I will bless you and praise your name forever and ever. Great is the Lord . . . " (145:2-3, ESV). Two things really stand out to me in these first three verses. First, notice the words "I will." David intentionally turned his thoughts from what was going on in his life to recognizing and acknowledging God's greatness. And look how often he did this—every day! We have such a propensity to drown in life's circumstances that we can easily forget who God is and how active He is in our lives. David purposefully and daily turned his eyes from his situations and on to God's goodness and activity.

#2 Psalm 145:4-7

David challenges us to talk to our family and friends about the good things God does. He even encourages us to celebrate His blessings! David also says he *meditates* on God's activity. What if we took extended times to think about His goodness? God provides for us and sustains us every day, and we should take time to acknowledge Him and all of His blessings.

#3 Psalm 145:8-12

David faced many difficulties during his life—betrayal, failure, battles, and loss. I'm sure he felt overwhelmed by those challenges, just like we do. However, we read how David recounts God's mercy and love. Throughout the Psalms, we see David telling God about his problems, and then switching his focus back on to who God is and what He does. What if we switched where our thoughts are abiding—from our circumstances, to His love? In John 15, Jesus invites us to abide in His love. Abiding in His love is a much better place to dwell than in our challenges. When we live aware of His love, we grow more and more secure in His promise to provide for us and walk with us every step of the way. Circumstances can overwhelm, but Jesus offers peace that isn't dependent upon an easy life.

> When you recognize His presence and activity, you can abide in His unfailing love and not your ever-changing, overwhelming circumstances.

#4 Psalm 145:13

David reminded himself of the eternal reality of God. We exist in a certain time and space, causing us to be limited in our view of the circumstances we are walking through. God sees so much more than we could even imagine. He sees from the beginning of time on earth to the very end of the current age and well beyond. (Mind blowing!) This should change how we engage with Him.

#5 Psalm 145:13-20
These Scriptures give us a beautiful glimpse into the heart of God for His children. He is gracious, compassionate, slow to anger, and rich in love. When we remember His character and His deep love for us, our conversations with Him are dramatically different—instead of fret-filled prayers, we pray faith-filled ones.

#6 Psalm 145:21
David begins and ends this psalm with praise! We can only praise Him when we *remember* His character and acknowledge His activity.

Friends, let's take the time to turn toward Him, give Him our full attention, and *remember* who He is and all He does! When you recognize His presence and activity, you can abide in His unfailing love and not your ever-changing, overwhelming circumstances. This shift of focus requires diligence, but it can be made when we intentionally remind ourselves of His character and activity. This week's prayer prompts are focused on *remembering*! I pray you experience indescribable peace as you spend time reflecting on Him and all He has done for you.

DAY 1
PRAYER PROMPT

READ PSALM 103

We need to consistently remind ourselves of who God is. After reading this passage of Scripture, take some time to personalize the specific verses. (For example, "God, thank You for redeeming my life with your steadfast love and mercy. Thank You for removing my sins as far as the east is from the west . . . ") Notice David says, "Forget not all his benefits." Think about His character and ask the Lord to help you remember who He is. Write out the aspects of God which you need to remember most right now.

_____

_____

_____

_____

_____

_____

_____

_____

_____

_____

_____

_____

_____

_____

_____

_____

_____

_____

_____

DAY 2
PRAYER PROMPT

READ DEUTERONOMY 8

As you read through Deuteronomy 8, write out what the Lord instructed the Israelites to remember. Then read it again and take note of the dangers of forgetting what the Lord has done. What happens to our hearts when we forget what God does for us?

Take a few minutes to recognize the good things in your life right now. James tells us every good thing is a gift from God. When we take time to notice the good, we are acknowledging God's activity in our lives. Write out how thankful you are for all of the ways He is providing for you right now. Make a fresh commitment to remembering and meditating on His goodness.

_____

_____

_____

_____

_____

_____

_____

_____

_____

_____

_____

_____

_____

_____

_____

_____

_____

DAY 3
PRAYER PROMPT

READ MARK 8:14-21

Jesus said, "Don't you remember?" The disciples had witnessed Jesus feeding thousands of people with just a couple loaves of bread and a few fish. And they were worried about not having enough bread? Really? While my first reaction to the disciples is critical, I realize I can be exactly the same way. God provides in one setting, but in a new situation I'm anxious. Jesus doesn't want us to worry every time we walk into a new set of circumstances. He wants us to remember how powerful, good, faithful, and loving He is. Think back over your life and recall the times when God provided what was needed. Remember who He is and take some time to express your gratitude and your trust in Him. What current circumstances are heaviest on your heart right now? How can remembering what God has done before (either in His Word or in your life) help you to trust Him in this situation?

_____

_____

_____

_____

_____

_____

_____

_____

_____

_____

_____

_____

_____

_____

DAY 4
PRAYER PROMPT

READ ROMANS 8:26-39

This is a power-packed portion of Scripture. These verses help us to remember how God is for us and nothing can separate us from Him and His purposes in our lives. Take some time to read through this passage slowly and in several translations. Then take note of the phrases that stand out to you. Write those verses in your journal and the truths you need to remember right now. Thank Him for reminding you of these truths.

_____

_____

_____

_____

_____

_____

_____

_____

_____

_____

_____

_____

_____

_____

_____

_____

_____

_____

_____

DAY 5
PRAYER PROMPT

READ REVELATION 21:1-7

Because we live in such a temporal world, we need to remind ourselves of the reality of Heaven and our everlasting Father. God is in complete control and He is preparing a place for us to dwell with Him throughout all eternity. In your journal, write out what this passage tells you about God and the future you will have with Him. Ask Him to help you remember the significance of this passage and to see your current circumstances in light of eternity.

_____

_____

_____

_____

_____

_____

_____

_____

_____

_____

_____

_____

_____

_____

_____

_____

_____

END-OF-THE-WEEK JOURNAL PROMPTS

1) Which portion of Scripture stood out to you this week and why?

_____

_____

_____

_____

_____

_____

2) When do you find yourself "abiding in your circumstances" more than abiding in God's Word and His love?

_____

_____

_____

_____

_____

_____

3) What happens to your emotions when your thoughts are more focused on your difficulties than on the character and love of God?

_____

_____

_____

_____

_____

_____

4) What changed in your attitude when you took time to express your gratitude to God?

_____

_____

_____

_____

_____

_____

5) How can you celebrate His goodness and activity in your life and the lives of your family and friends?

_____

_____

_____

_____

_____

_____

6) How do your prayers shift when you intentionally start your time of prayer with remembering who God is and what He is doing in your life?

_____

_____

_____

_____

_____

_____

LISTENING DILIGENTLY TO HIS WORD

WEEK THREE

LISTENING

ISAIAH 55:1-3, PSALM 81:6-16, MATTHEW 17:1-5

Is prayer really two-way conversation? If it is, how does God speak to us? Should we expect to hear His audible voice? Do we anticipate goosebumps or something supernatural to happen in order to know when God is speaking to us? Or do we even expect to hear from Him at all?

Several years ago, I began to notice the passages of Scripture where God tells us to "listen" to Him. Isaiah 55 was one of the first to really stand out to me. It is basically an entire chapter imploring us to pay attention to Him. He says, "Listen diligently to me, and eat what is good and delight yourselves in rich food. Incline your ear and come to me; hear, that your soul may live," (verses 2-3). In this same chapter, He invites us to seek Him and call upon Him (verse 6). It is clear from this portion of Scripture that God wants us to pray, and it involves *listening* as well as *seeking* His activity in our lives.

Friends, prayer is definitely two-way communication. God has given us His Word, and it is the clearest, most direct way He communicates with us! We are so privileged to have multiple copies available to us. We have hard copies to hold in our hands and highlight with markers. We have electronic versions on our phones and laptops to access at any time. We can even listen to His Word on a free app from our phones while we are getting ready in the morning or driving home from work.

The Bible isn't just a collection of stories and good advice—it is *God's Word*. He tells us His Word is alive and active—it isn't stale and static. Hebrews 4:12 says it this way: "For the Word of God is living and active, sharper than any two-edged sword, piercing to the division of soul and of spirit, of joints and of marrow, and discerning the thoughts and intentions of the heart." Just think about all that means! He wants to speak deep into our souls and adjust our thoughts, emotions, and intentions. His voice can realign everything inside our hearts and minds. Since His Word is *living*, verses we've read for years can take on a whole new, deeper meaning for a situation we are currently walking through.

> He wants to speak deep into our souls and adjust our thoughts, emotions, and intentions. His voice can realign everything inside our hearts and minds.

As we are faithful to read His Word, He is faithful to speak to us! He has so much to say, and we need to learn how to *listen*, not just simply read. We have to be willing to turn aside from distractions, remember Who we are listening to, and pay close attention to what He has to say.

We often talk about Bible reading and prayer as if they are two completely separate activities. We know they are both healthy spiritual disciplines. However, we may not engage them as connectedly as we should. I spent years reading the Bible and gaining head knowledge. However, when I started to pray, I simply jumped in with what was on my heart, giving little to no thought about what I just read in His Word. But something shifted dramatically when I started to view His Word as the God-side of a two-way conversation.

Take some time to read Isaiah 55:2-3, Psalm 81:6-16, and Matthew 17:5 before you look at the following things I share from the passages. As you read, consider how much richer our prayer life could be if we were as committed to *listening* as we are to *asking*.

#1 Isaiah 55:1-2

He invites those who are thirsty to come and discover something so much better than anything we buy or work for. It seems He knows we are searching for something, and we are looking in places that will never satisfy—our work and our things. He wants us to experience His presence and activity, and it can only be found as we engage with Him through prayer and listening carefully to what He has to say.

#2 Isaiah 55:2-3

He tells us how listening to Him will be "delightful" and "satisfying." He says, "Listen diligently to me, and eat what is good, and delight yourselves in rich food. Incline your ear, and come to me; hear, that your soul may live." Wow, just wow! This doesn't sound like God wants to be silent! He has vital things to say to us, things that are good and delightful! Things that will satisfy the deepest parts of who we are. And it requires our diligence—did you catch that? We need to be tenacious. We should ruthlessly carve out time, turn away from all distractions, open His Word and *listen*, not just read, but really *listen*.

#3 Isaiah 55:3b

As we listen to Him, He will help us understand His covenant of love, just as He did with David (who is described as a man after God's own heart). David believed God's Word, and trusted wholeheartedly in God's unfailing love. When we really *listen* to God's Truth, we grow in our understanding of His love for us. Understanding how He feels about us builds trust and strengthens our faith. Knowing He loves us and acts for our best interest helps us to rest in Him, even when we don't understand what is going on around us.

> We should ruthlessly carve out time, turn away from all distractions, open His Word and listen, not just read, but really listen.

#4 Psalm 81:8

Can't you just hear the heart of God in His urgent plea? "Oh, that my people would listen to me, that Israel would walk in my ways! I would soon subdue their enemies . . . " He has so much for us, but we will never experience His activity unless we first take time to listen.

#5 Psalm 81:11-12

He doesn't force us to listen. When we aren't listening, we don't have the opportunity to follow Him or gain His perspective. He allows us to walk down paths that are unfulfilling and even destructive. We get stuck in the emotional turmoil of the circumstances surrounding us and miss the most important thing—what God is saying. He wants to lead us through the situation, teaching us deep truths along the way, but this requires good listening skills and right responses. (We will look at the importance of responding in the next session.)

#6 Matthew 17:1-5

This is a fascinating portion of Scripture! Not only did Moses and Elijah show up long after their earthly lives ended, but God spoke audibly. Here we get a unique glimpse of an eternal reality. Two individuals who lived in different eras are alive, together, and interacting with Jesus! Wow! Then Peter, James, and John, audibly heard Father God say, "This is my beloved Son, with whom I am well pleased; *listen* to Him." God spoke, and what did He say? He validated Jesus as His Son, and then told us to *listen* to Him! As I read those audible words of God, I'm challenged to ask myself this question, "Am I really *listening* to the Words of Jesus or am I just reading them?"

Isaiah 55, Psalm 81, and Matthew 17 are three very different passages of Scripture. Yet each one gives us a clear understanding of the value of listening to God. He has so much to say, and what He says is life-giving! I want to challenge you to focus on really *listening* to God in the coming week. Of course, you should continue to ask for Him to work on your behalf, but intentionally listen more than you ask. I'm excited for you to hear what He has to say specifically to you!

DAY 1
PRAYER PROMPT

READ PSALM 81:8-16

Verse 8 gives us an amazing glimpse into the heart of God, "Hear, O my people, while I admonish you! O Israel, if you would but listen to me!" Do you think He could be saying the same thing to you? Repent for those times when you've rushed through prayers, without giving much thought to what He wants to say to you.

Write out the benefits of listening to God as described in these verses. Read verse 16 carefully and consider what God is saying in this verse. Take time to really *listen* to what the Lord wants to say to you from this psalm. Write out what you "hear." Then write a fresh commitment to "listen" to Him more than you make requests.

_____

_____

_____

_____

_____

_____

_____

_____

_____

_____

_____

_____

_____

_____

_____

DAY 2
PRAYER PROMPT

READ ISAIAH 55

Write out those things you learn about God in this chapter. Read carefully the invitation found in verses 1-3. Write out your response to His offer. Consider what He is inviting you to experience and how He will respond when you listen diligently to Him. Ask yourself if you are looking for fulfillment in things that will never satisfy. Then take some time to repent for spending more effort on things that won't satisfy. Ask Him what He wants you to learn from Isaiah 55—then write out what you hear Him say.

_____

_____

_____

_____

_____

_____

_____

_____

_____

_____

_____

_____

_____

_____

_____

_____

_____

_____

_____

DAY 3
PRAYER PROMPT

REREAD ISAIAH 55

List all of the benefits of listening to God found in Isaiah 55:2, 3, 7, 8-9, 10-11, 12. Consider what you could experience by *listening more diligently* to Him. Which Scripture stands out the most to you in this chapter? Write it out, think about it, pray it, and respond to it.

_____

_____

_____

_____

_____

_____

_____

_____

_____

_____

_____

_____

_____

_____

_____

_____

_____

_____

_____

_____

_____

_____

_____

_____

DAY 4
PRAYER PROMPT

READ LUKE 8:4-15

This is a well-known parable of Jesus. The seed in this story represents the Word of God. The types of soil represent the people and how they *listen*. The path represents those who listen to the Word of God and then allow the lies of the enemy to speak louder—robbing them of the truth. The rocky soil represents those who hear, but don't take enough time in the Word for it to take root in their hearts, so they easily fall away when life gets rough. The thorny soil represents those who hear, but are listening more to the lure of *stuff* and the pleasures of life than to the Word of God. The seed doesn't have the opportunity to produce fruit in their lives. The good soil represents those who listen really well. They take time to let His Word sink deep in their hearts and minds, and it changes how they live.

Ask God how He would describe the soil of your heart. What are you listening to most closely—the lies of the enemy, your problems, the lure of *stuff*, or His Word? What things do you need to adjust to listen more carefully to His Word? Make a fresh commitment to take the time and make the effort to listen really well. Write out your commitment.

_____

_____

_____

_____

_____

_____

_____

_____

_____

_____

DAY 5
PRAYER PROMPT

READ PSALM 19:7-11

After reading Psalm 19:7-11, list all of the benefits of listening to God's Word as described in this psalm. Then open a Bible app on your phone and listen to Psalm 19 being read aloud. Listen for what the Lord says to you as you hear this psalm. Take note of what stands out to you and then respond to Him.

_____

_____

_____

_____

_____

_____

_____

_____

_____

_____

_____

_____

_____

_____

_____

_____

_____

_____

END-OF-THE-WEEK JOURNAL PROMPTS

1) Which verse from this week's devotions impacted you the most and why?

_____

_____

_____

_____

_____

_____

2) Describe which day of journaling was most impactful for you.

_____

_____

_____

_____

_____

_____

3) How do one-sided conversations make you feel? What do you miss when you engage in prayer like it is only about you making your requests known to God?

_____

_____

_____

_____

_____

_____

4) What did you learn about the character of God in the Scripture reading this week?

_____

_____

_____

_____

_____

_____

5) Has your prayer life changed by focusing more on listening than asking? If so, how has it changed?

_____

_____

_____

_____

_____

_____

6) What are some practical ways you can engage Scripture as the God-side of the conversation during your times of prayer?

_____

_____

_____

_____

_____

_____

ENGAGING WITH GOD

RESPONDING TO HIS VOICE

RESPONDING

ISAIAH 55:6-13

Have you ever wondered how you can truly reflect the character of Christ? I certainly have, and to be honest, at times, it seems almost impossible. Our natural responses are so far from righteous. Even after we experience salvation, we can find ourselves stuck in thought patterns and behaviors that are unhealthy and nonproductive.

We experience salvation when we hear the Good News and *respond*. The moment we believe Jesus is the Son of God and repent of our sins, we receive salvation. We don't earn it or deserve it, in faith, we simply accept it. And what an incredible gift it is—freedom from sin and the opportunity to enjoy a relationship with our Creator!

Responding to God is always a catalyst for transformation. God has so much for us as His children, but our ongoing *responses* to Him determine the quality and fruitfulness of our lives. I can see this so clearly as I look back over my life. I grew up in a wonderful family who faithfully lived the Gospel in front of me every day. I experienced salvation and baptism at a young age. But even with all of these advantages, I experienced a shallow, unproductive life. As a young woman, I struggled with pride, insecurity, self-centered thoughts, and wrong attitudes.

Transformation began when a friend invited me to attend an interdenominational Bible study group. These women had an intimate knowledge of Scripture, and their discussions centered around the ways God's Word applied specifically to them as young moms. I was mesmerized by their conversations and loved listening in to their discussions! The book we discussed required hours of study each week. As a mom with two little boys, a toddler and a preschooler, I didn't have very many moments without interruptions. In order to prepare for the group discussions, I needed to create some quiet moments in our house. So we started the quiet hour. When our little guy was napping, our four-year-old could read, color, play with Legos, whatever he liked, as long as he was quiet. (Being a reflective little soul, I think he enjoyed the quiet hour as much as I did.) This time quickly became one of my favorite parts of the day. I was able to listen to God's Word and process what I was reading as I worked through the material.

> Our ongoing responses to Him determine the quality and fruitfulness of our lives.

Before this season in my life, I read my Bible and prayed, but it wasn't a genuine two-way conversation—Him speaking and me responding to what I heard. It was simply an activity I checked off of my "to-do list." I knew there were rules to follow, and I tried to live a good life and be the best wife and mom I could. It wasn't as easy as I thought it would be. I was constantly dealing with my *stuff*—like selfishness, narrow perspectives, and wrong attitudes. (My poor husband!)

However, as I took time to really listen to His Word, the Holy Spirit helped me to see how I was allowing my sinful nature to lead my attitudes and behaviors. Yes, I was saved, but I was far from reflecting the character of Jesus. The wonderful thing is—the listening didn't just point out my faults, it also brought kind correction and clear instruction, which began to reshape my thoughts and motives.

This is when real transformation began in my life! Thankfully, He's still not done working on me—there is still a ton of room for improvement. Even after decades of listening and responding, I'm far from accurately representing my Savior every moment of the day. Thankfully, He continues to speak to me as I take the time to listen. Then I have a choice to respond. *Responding* to His voice always brings good changes in my heart and mind and greater fruitfulness in my relationships and work.

Here are just a few ways listening diligently prompts me to *respond*:

» Remembering His power and faithfulness encourages me to choose faith over fear.
» Hearing His correction helps me to recognize when I am self-focused, and encourages me to turn my attention to those around me.

» Recognizing His sovereignty inspires me to submit to His will instead of kicking and screaming to get my way.
» Gaining His perspective gives me wisdom.
» Receiving His love helps me to rest in His provision.
» Learning the Truth helps me to recognize the lies of the enemy.
» Knowing His intentions are always good helps me to trust Him, even if I don't like or understand what is going on around me.

Two-way communication with God involves turning, remembering, listening, and *responding*. Prayer becomes transformational when we take time to *respond*. Let's take a look at what God says about responding to His Word in Isaiah 55:6-13.

#1 Isaiah 55:6-7
In these two verses, God invites us to seek Him and call upon Him. This is our side of prayer. However, He goes on to talk about how we should respond to what He has to say. We should turn from the things that don't please Him. His Word will shine a spotlight on those things which need adjusting. When we repent, God will have compassion on us and will forgive us. He is never harsh or critical—" . . . let him return to the LORD, that he may have compassion on him, and to our God, for he will abundantly pardon," (Isaiah 55:7, ESV). His kindness leads us to repentance, and repentance leads us to life!

Oh friend, repentance is such an important, but often neglected part of prayer. It's so important to remember that repentance isn't just a one-time act, it is the ongoing posture of our heart. As we are faithful to draw close to Him, *in love* He will show us our sin and give us the strength to turn away from those destructive things.

#2 Isaiah 55:8-9
God's thoughts and ways are so much higher than ours! Even as believers, we have a very limited understanding of spiritual realities. In addition to our incomplete knowledge, we live in a world where God is largely disregarded. The ways of our society are quite contrary to the ways of God. Since we live in this world (and our world speaks so loudly), we can easily listen to the wrong voices and slip into incorrect thinking. This always leads to wrong behaviors and brokenness. I don't know about you, but I need to be in His Word every day if I want any chance of aligning my thoughts and ways to His. When I truly listen to Scripture as God's side of the conversation, I have a much clearer understanding of truth. Only by hearing God's perspective can I have right responses.

#3 Isaiah 55:10-11

When God speaks to us through His Word, it is for a specific purpose. His Word waters us and nourishes us. In verses 1-3, God invites us to come to Him and listen diligently, and when we do, we find satisfaction for our souls. Nothing will satisfy our souls like genuinely hearing Him speak to us. As we receive from Him, we discover His purposes for our lives. His Word produces actions in our lives which enable His purposes to be done here on earth. (Pretty incredible!)

#4 Isaiah 55:12-13

Oh, how I love these two verses! Listening to Him and responding to His Word will bring great joy and peace in our lives! Instead of our lives being full of "thorns and briers," we will see health and growth in our hearts, minds, attitudes, relationships, and work.

Isaiah 55 helps us to understand the incredible, numerous gifts of two-way engagement with the Lord. Our thoughts and behaviors begin to change and we begin to reflect His characteristics. Our lives become more and more fruitful. The challenges we face even begin to dim in comparison to His sweet presence and activity. This is a life-long adventure of ongoing listening and responding.

> God invites us to come to Him and listen diligently, and when we do, we find satisfaction for our souls.

I pray that this week you experience the benefits God lists in Isaiah as you listen diligently and *respond* to His voice. May you find new fulfillment, purpose, joy, and peace. May your perspective be adjusted to be more in line with His thoughts. May your attitudes, words, and behaviors reflect Him more accurately. I pray you experience renewed fruitfulness in your relationships and work.

DAY 1
PRAYER PROMPT

PSALM 139:23-24

Often, we find ourselves wanting God's direction or provision in our lives, but seldom do we seek His correction. Without this kind of openness with the Lord, we will never experience growth. David invited God to shine a light on his heart and thoughts and behaviors. He asked God to lead him to transformation. Take some time to rewrite this prayer in your own words, and give God the opportunity to respond. He may bring to mind corrective Scripture passages you've read recently or an encounter when you responded inappropriately. Allow the Holy Spirit to point out anything in you that grieves the Lord. It is His kindness that leads us to repentance. Write out what you want to say in response to Him.

DAY 2
PRAYER PROMPT

READ DEUTERONOMY 30

Verses 11-20 in Deuteronomy 30 describe the choice we have to respond to God's Word. Read it slowly and allow the Holy Spirit to point out something specific to you. Write out those things that stand out to you in this passage. Take time to respond to those verses.

Ask the Lord to help you to understand what it looks like for you to practically:

» Love the Lord your God
» Obey His voice
» Hold fast to Him

Reread verses 8-10 and write out the blessings you will experience when you choose to turn to the Lord with all your heart.

_____

_____

_____

_____

_____

_____

_____

_____

_____

_____

_____

_____

_____

_____

DAY 3
PRAYER PROMPT

READ COLOSSIANS 3:1-4:6

This passage of Scripture starts off by challenging us to "set our minds on things above" (3:2). It goes on to describe *our responsibility* to "put to death" the destructive things in our lives and to "put on" the character of Christ. While salvation is a free gift from God, we clearly see our need to *respond correctly to His instructions* if we want to experience the abundant life Christ offers us. As you read through this passage, listen closely for what the Lord would say to you. When you hear His voice, write out what you hear Him say and how you will choose to respond. Pray for the Lord to help you "put on" the right things today!

_____

_____

_____

_____

_____

_____

_____

_____

_____

_____

_____

_____

_____

_____

_____

_____

_____

_____

DAY 4
PRAYER PROMPT

READ PSALM 19

This passage lists the incredible benefits of listening to God's Word, but it also gives us *instruction on how to respond*. Reread verses 11-14 and write them out as your own prayer. Give the Lord time to evaluate your thoughts and words. I know this can be painful, but as we allow Him access into the "meditation of our hearts," our responses to what He reveals can bring incredible transformation. Try to be transparent in His presence. Remember His goal is to revive your soul, give you wisdom, bring joy to your heart, and provide light for each step of the way. Write out what you hear Him say and how you want to respond.

_____

_____

_____

_____

_____

_____

_____

_____

_____

_____

_____

_____

_____

_____

_____

_____

DAY 5
PRAYER PROMPT

READ PSALM 138:8-139:18

Write out what these verses tell you specifically about God in relationship with you. Then read the last two verses in Psalm 139. How did David's understanding of God's character impact his ability to pray such a vulnerable prayer? As you think about these verses, how do you want to respond to God—the One who created you, knows you, is with you, and has plans for you?

_____

_____

_____

_____

_____

_____

_____

_____

_____

_____

_____

_____

_____

_____

_____

_____

_____

_____

_____

_____

_____

END-OF-THE-WEEK JOURNAL PROMPTS

1) Which portion of Scripture stood out to you this week and why?

_____

_____

_____

_____

_____

_____

_____

2) Describe the value of taking time to respond to what you hear God saying. How can this be incorporated into your times of prayer?

_____

_____

_____

_____

_____

_____

_____

3) How are your responses to God linked to the transformation of your character?

_____

_____

_____

_____

_____

_____

_____

_____

4) Since God's thoughts and ways are so different from yours, describe the value of reading and listening to His Word. How can the voice of the world drown out God's voice and impact our responses?

_____

_____

_____

_____

_____

_____

_____

_____

5) Which daily prayer prompt or journaling exercise impacted you the most this week and why?

_____

_____

_____

_____

_____

_____

_____

_____

ASKING FOR HIS INVOLVEMENT

WEEK FIVE

ASKING

MATTHEW 6-7

Does God really want us to ask for His help? The answer is YES!

Scripture is full of beautiful prayers asking God for his intervention. Prayers like this one:

"Make me to know your ways, O Lord;
teach me your paths.
Lead me in your truth and teach me,
for you are the God of my salvation;
for you I wait all the day long."
–Psalm 25:4-5 (ESV)

Not only can we read prayers of requests throughout Scripture, Jesus teaches us *how* to ask in Matthew 6-7. The well-known Lord's Prayer is tucked in to this part of Scripture. We learn so much about how to communicate with our Heavenly Father from the words that follow, "Pray then like this" in Matthew 6:9. Jesus couldn't be more direct. He is explaining to us *how* to make our requests known to God. Yet, we learn additional things about prayer from other verses in these two chapters as well. So take a few minutes to read Matthew chapters 6-7 before you finish reading this session. Highlight the verses that speak directly about prayer.

Let's consider those things Jesus wants us to know from this passage about making our requests known to God:

#1 Matthew 6:1

The first verse in chapter 6 gives us some important insights. Jesus tells us all true spiritual pursuits must be done for an audience of One, and not for the applause of people. Whether we are giving money, praying, or fasting, it needs to be done *in secret* for our Father in Heaven—for Him alone. (Matthew 6:4, 6, 18) If we do these things to be noticed by others, their recognition will be the only reward we receive. Prayer should be fueled by the desire to connect with God so we can know Him, express our love for Him, and honor Him with our lives.

#2 Matthew 6:5, 7

As a child, I didn't have an accurate view of making our requests known to God. For some unknown reason, I thought we should be proper and keep our true emotions hidden during times of personal prayer. I still don't know why I thought this. Maybe I was simply afraid or embarrassed to admit my true feelings to God. And public prayers were quite intimidating. In church settings, I witnessed adults praying loud, demonstrative prayers (in King James English, by the way). These misconceptions followed me into my young adult years. My prayer life was rather shallow and routine. I rarely opened up and shared honestly with God in personal times of prayer, and I continued to be intimidated to pray aloud in group settings.

> Honest, humble communication with God is the path to growing intimacy with Him.

Friends, Jesus wants us to know that we don't have to be stoic, rote, and proper when we pray. Nor do we have to be loud, impressive, or repetitive with our prayers. We can simply tell Him our deepest thoughts and ask Him to meet our every need. Honest, humble communication with God is the path to growing intimacy with Him.

#3 Matthew 6:9-13

Jesus gave us a pattern for prayer. He tells us to start our prayers by honoring God and asking for His will to be done in our lives. Then He instructs us to ask for:

1) Our needs to be met,
2) Forgiveness and His help to forgive others,

3) His help in fighting the temptations that come into our lives, and

4) His deliverance from evil.

These four areas cover our physical needs, relationships with others, temptations with sin, and the ongoing battle with evil. Essentially we can make requests for all of the things that touch our lives.

#4 Matthew 6:15

Immediately after telling us *how* to pray, Jesus emphasizes the importance of forgiveness. He even says if we don't forgive others, we can't be forgiven. Look back at the Lord's prayer (Matthew 6:9-13). It is a prayer of honoring God and making our requests known. The only instruction Jesus gives us which requires action on our part is, "forgive us our debts, *as we also have forgiven our debtors*." Friends, it is vital for us to forgive those who have wronged us. Our prayer life will be negatively impacted if we don't.

Our choice to forgive others reveals a recognition of our own sin and the need we have for God's mercy and grace. Refusing to forgive someone, even if we think their sin is greater than ours, exposes our pride and self-righteous attitudes. (I know, *ouch!*) James 4:6 tells us, "God opposes the proud, but gives grace to the humble." The choice to forgive humbly declares that God is our source for every need. Forgiveness reveals our trust and complete dependence on God. Deciding to forgive those who sin against us puts us in a right relationship with God by allowing God's grace to flow freely in our lives. And it is good for our hearts because it lessens the grip of the offense and releases us to live free from bitterness and anger.

#5 Matthew 6:16-18

Fasting (or giving something up) to have more time and focus on prayer pleases the heart of God. Jesus assumes we will fast, for He says, "*when* you fast," not "*if* you fast." Fasting says to the Lord, *I want Your intervention and purposes in this situation more than I want physical nourishment.* For a determined amount of time, we can give up food (or certain foods or specific meals). This is an effective way to demonstrate our desire for God's intervention and to make our requests known to Him.

Remember, Jesus says it is important to fast for an audience of One and not for the recognition of others. When fasting is a completely private matter—just for your Father, He will reward you!

#6 Matthew 6:25-34

In this passage, Jesus tells us not to be anxious about anything. Just earlier in chapter six, Jesus says to ask God for our daily needs this way: "Give us this day our daily bread." He isn't saying we can only ask for food; we should ask God to provide for every need—physical, emotional, relational, occupational, or spiritual. However, I think it is important to note, especially when it comes to anxiety, that Jesus says, "Give us **this** day our **daily** bread."

Jesus tells us our Father knows what we need even before we ask (Matthew 6:8). He is aware of every detail of our lives. He promises to supply our every need as we rely on Him (Philippians 4:19). However, God typically meets needs as we have them—and not much before. Friends, we can only experience God's provision in the moment we are experiencing. When we try to live too far in the future, we will likely experience anxiety.

I've been challenged to focus the majority of my requests on the day in front of me, not next year. While He knows the future, we can only live in the current day. So rest in Him this moment and make your requests known for this day. Trust Him to supply what you need, when you need it. Jesus tells us not to worry about tomorrow. His provision will be there when we get there.

#7 Matthew 7:7-11

Jesus tells us to *ask*, *seek*, and *knock*. He wants us to make our requests known to the Father. And He promises, "Everyone who asks receives, and the one who seeks finds, and to the one who knocks it will be opened" (verse 8). He even says, "If you then who are evil, know how to give good gifts to your children, how much more will your Father who is in heaven give good things to those who ask him" (verse 11).

Never think you are bothering Him with your requests. It pleases His heart when you demonstrate your trust in Him by asking, seeking, and knocking. He wants you to keep asking! You can make a request known to Him every day for years—it reveals your faith in Him to respond.

As you pray this week, take time to turn away from distractions and shut yourself away with Him. Remember Who He is, listen diligently to His Word, take time to respond to what you hear Him saying, and *ask Him for what you need*! He invites us to seek Him and call upon Him. It pleases His heart when we rely on Him to provide for us and meet our needs.

DAY 1
PRAYER PROMPT

READ MATTHEW 6:25-34 AND MATTHEW 7:7-11

Write out what these passages tell you about your Heavenly Father. Then make a list of the things you are encouraged to do. Is there a situation (or situations) creating anxiety for you? How do these verses encourage you to engage with God? How can you adjust your thoughts about the situation to experience peace rather than fear? Write out the truths you need to remember on a notecard and keep it where you can read it throughout the day. Whenever you experience fear, read the card and ask God to help you rest in His care.

_____

_____

_____

_____

_____

_____

_____

_____

_____

_____

_____

_____

_____

_____

_____

_____

_____

_____

_____

DAY 2
PRAYER PROMPT

READ 1 THESSALONIANS 5:17

How can we pray without ceasing? Dr. Carolyn Tennant, one of my seminary professors, taught me about the concept of "breath prayers." When something is heavy on our hearts, we can make our requests to God throughout the day with a simple, short prayer—the length of a breath. When my father was suffering and close to death, my breath prayer became, "Be merciful." When a close friend desperately needed a job, my prayer was "open a door." When I was walking through a deep disappointment, my breath prayer was, "Heal my heart."

Is there something heavy on your heart today? Take some time to tell Him all about it in great detail. And then summarize it to a simple statement and pray it throughout your day.

_____

_____

_____

_____

_____

_____

_____

_____

_____

_____

_____

_____

_____

_____

_____

_____

DAY 3
PRAYER PROMPT

READ EXODUS 16:11-30

Consider how God cared for the Israelites with *daily* manna, and what He was teaching them in Exodus 16.

I tend to focus on the future—how things can be improved next time I take on that task, or what God might have for me in the next season of life, or . . . (the list goes on and on). The problem with living too far in the future is that I will either experience discontentment with my current reality or worry about what is to come. And I miss the beauty of the moment I am living. Maybe, like me, you spend excessive time praying for things that are far out in the future. What would it look like for you to focus your prayers on the day that is right in front of you? I've been challenged with this as well. When my requests are focused more on the "daily bread," or the step that is right in front of me, I experience incredible peace and have clarity and help with the day I am living.

Write out your prayer requests for the things you are facing right now, what you need for the step you are on (not the entire staircase). Ask the Lord to help you not to worry about the future, but to live fully in this day by experiencing the "daily bread" He has for you right now.

DAY 4
PRAYER PROMPT

READ MATTHEW 18:21-35

After reading the passage in Matthew 18, reread point #4 from this week's session. Then honestly search your heart and ask yourself if there is someone you are refusing to forgive. I know this may be painful, but in the long run, it will be more painful for you if you try to sidestep the need to forgive someone. Your relationship with God is in the balance.

We forgive because we are forgiven. Here are a few things to remember about forgiveness:

Forgiveness IS NOT:

1) Denying or forgetting the offense
2) Living without boundaries with the one who hurt you

Forgiveness IS:

1) Choosing not to get even
2) Choosing to give the person good, not evil
3) Trusting God with the outcome

This is so very important! Please don't refuse to forgive! Your prayers are negatively impacted by a refusal to forgive. Pray and ask the Lord to help you. Then, if you still can't seem to forgive, talk to someone who is mature in their faith for advice and prayer.

_____

_____

_____

_____

_____

_____

_____

_____

DAY 5
PRAYER PROMPT

READ PSALM 143

Notice how David communicates with God in this Psalm: he begins by asking God to hear and answer him. He goes on to describe his current situation of being exhausted from battle. Then David says he meditates on all God has done for him in the past. Again, he begs God to answer quickly and not to ignore him. In verse eight, David asks God to reveal His steadfast love and declares his trust in Him. He clearly asks God to lead him, to teach him to do God's will, and for God to destroy his enemies.

Write out your requests to God by using the pattern laid out in this Psalm:

- » ask God to hear and answer you,
- » tell Him about your situation,
- » think about what God has done in the past,
- » declare your trust in Him,
- » ask Him to reveal His love, to lead you, and to give you victory in the situations you are facing.

_____

_____

_____

_____

_____

_____

_____

_____

_____

_____

_____

END-OF-THE-WEEK JOURNAL PROMPTS

1) Jesus teaches us a lot about prayer in Matthew 6-7. What stands out to you the most in these two chapters about asking?

_____

_____

_____

_____

_____

_____

_____

_____

_____

2) How is worry lessened when you focus more on the step in front of you rather than the entire staircase?

_____

_____

_____

_____

_____

_____

_____

_____

_____

3) When a situation is heavy on your heart, how can a "breath prayer" keep you in communication with your Father throughout the day? How can that type of prayer strengthen your faith and lessen worry?

_____

_____

_____

_____

_____

_____

_____

_____

_____

_____

4) Read Matthew 7:7-11. How do these verses make you feel about making your requests known to God?

_____

_____

_____

_____

_____

_____

_____

_____

_____

_____

WAITING ON HIS RESPONSE

WEEK SIX

WAITING

JOHN 11:1-45

Waiting is rarely fun (unless you have a really good cup of coffee ☺). We simply do not like to wait. Impatience can be seen on roadways, in grocery store lines, doctor's offices, and basically anywhere there are unwanted, delayed responses. While we may not enjoy waiting, it is an important part of faith. Actually, faith requires waiting.

In John 11, we read about Martha, Mary, and Lazarus. While this is the account of Jesus raising Lazarus from the dead, it is also a story of praying and waiting. Take some time to read John 11:1-45 and put yourself in the place of Martha and Mary. Think about what they must have thought and felt at each stage of this situation. Then consider these seven things we can learn from this passage about praying and waiting for God to respond.

> While we may not enjoy waiting, it is an important part of faith. Actually, faith requires waiting.

#1 John 11:3-4

Martha and Mary sent word to Jesus about Lazarus being ill. The sisters knew Jesus could heal their brother and they expected Him to respond to their request for help. Since there were no cell phones, they had to send a messenger. They didn't know if Jesus received the message or how He would respond when He heard Lazarus was sick. However, these verses give us the other side of the story—Jesus heard and immediately knew how He was going to respond.

#2 John 11:5-6

I find the placement of these two verses very intriguing. "Now Jesus loved Martha and her sister and Lazarus. So, when he heard that Lazarus was ill, he stayed two days longer in the place where he was." Jesus loved them, and yet He chose not to respond right away. (I know, *what?!*) We would think if He loved them He would drop everything and respond right away, but He intentionally waited to respond.

#3 John 11:14

Martha and Mary only saw what was happening right in front of them. They had no way of knowing what Jesus was planning. They walked through the death of their brother and it was very painful. They experienced intense sorrow in the waiting because they didn't understand what Jesus was planning.

#4 John 11:21-22, 32, 37

Everyone involved in the situation had a preconceived idea about how and when Jesus should have responded.

#5 John 11:25-27

In the waiting, Jesus told Martha, "I am the *resurrection and the life!*" I'm sure in this state of grief, she understood the truth of resurrection on a deeper level than if He had said it at any other time. The turmoil created by waiting for God to respond has a way of breaking up the soil of our hearts and helps us to receive new levels of understanding. He revealed an incredible truth to Martha while she was waiting for Him to respond.

#6 John 11:32-35

Even though Jesus knew He was about to raise Lazarus from the dead, He understood the emotions they were experiencing. He not only understood their sorrow, He experienced it and wept with them.

#7 John 11:14-15, 40-42

The waiting was all about their faith—*that they may believe*! Interestingly, it wasn't just about Martha's and Mary's faith, it was about the faith of everyone who was watching them wait on Jesus. Their friends who came to comfort them knew that they were close to Jesus, and they were waiting to see how He would respond.

APPLYING THESE LESSONS TO OUR OWN LIVES

What incredible lessons this passage holds about waiting on God to respond to our prayers! So, friend, if God seems slow in responding to something you are praying for, let's apply these seven things to your situation:

#1

Be assured that Jesus has heard your prayer and He knows exactly how He is going to respond to your need. It may be a very long time before He makes His plans known to you, but be assured He has a plan. He is working behind the scenes for your good and His glory.

> Be assured that Jesus has heard your prayer and He knows exactly how He is going to respond to your need.

#2

He loves you and He has your best interest at heart. If there is a delay, you can know it is on purpose and it is prompted by His love for you. You can trust His love!

#3

When God doesn't "seem to be responding" to our prayers, we can feel all sorts of negative emotions—like disappointment, anxiety, frustration, and sadness. Realize the emotions you are experiencing are real, and you can tell Him how you feel. Martha and Mary wept as they ran to Jesus and told Him exactly how they felt. You can too.

#4

You undoubtedly have ideas about how and when God should handle the challenge you are facing. However, He may have bigger plans than you can even imagine. Plans that will glorify Himself, build your faith, and help others to see Him clearly. You can trust Him because God knows and sees more than you can even begin to understand.

#5

God has something to reveal to you in the waiting. Seek Him! Run after Him just like Martha and Mary did—be honest with Him and tell Him how you feel and then **listen to what He** has to say. Since He isn't here in person with us (like He was with Martha and Mary), we need to dig deep into the Word and trust Him to reveal Himself during this challenging season. He has things for you to learn in the waiting—things you might not be able to learn at other times.

> God has something to reveal to you in the waiting.

Remember, listening to Him through His Word is God's side of your prayer.

#6

Trust that Jesus is weeping with you—He understands what you are feeling and He is moved with compassion to respond in the best way, in the best time! We experience such comfort when we remember He loves us and He is there with us in the sorrow.

#7

Consider how this season of waiting is about your faith. He wants you to BELIEVE in who He is! And it is not just about your faith, it's also about those who are watching you wait on God. While it is a time for you to grow, it is also giving others the opportunity to see His activity in your life. Think about who is standing around you, knowing you are trusting God and waiting to see if and how He responds.

So, let's be encouraged! His delay doesn't mean what the enemy is most likely whispering in your ear. Things like,

- » He doesn't hear you
- » He doesn't love you
- » You are all alone
- » It is a hopeless situation
- » You are stuck in this waiting season indefinitely . . .

He loves you! He sees a much bigger picture than you can possibly imagine. You can trust that while His response may be different than what you are hoping for, it will be amazing—even if you don't understand "the amazing part" until you are with Him in Heaven. Be faithful to read His Word and expect Him to reveal more of Himself to you. Trust that He understands your brokenness over the situation. And know He is building your faith—and not just yours, but all those close to you as well. He has a plan—TRUST it!

Friend, faith *requires* waiting. Faith is believing He hears you when you pray. Faith is trusting He will respond. Faith is knowing He is at work, even when you don't see it. Faith is believing His plan is best, even if we don't understand it (or like it). Faith is willing to wait for the God who sees us, hears us, loves us, and wants what is best for us. So let's wait well.

DAY 1
PRAYER PROMPT

READ PSALM 13

Is there something you are praying specifically about and God seems to be slow in responding? (I can't imagine very many of us can say no to that question.) Pray again about the situation using Psalm 13 as a pattern for your prayer:

- » Tell Him honestly how you feel about His delay in responding,
- » Describe the situation to Him (even if you've done it many times before),
- » Declare your trust in the knowledge that He has heard your request and knows how He is going to respond, and
- » Remember how He loves you and how He has responded in the past.

_____

_____

_____

_____

_____

_____

_____

_____

_____

_____

_____

_____

_____

_____

DAY 2
PRAYER PROMPT

READ ISAIAH 55:8-9, PROVERBS 3:5-8

Since God's ways are so much different than our ways, we have to trust Him with all of our hearts. Proverbs 3:5-7 give us some great insights for engaging in those moments when we don't understand His delay in responding to our prayers. Rewrite these verses as a proclamation of your faith. Write out how you can acknowledge Him even as you wait on His response. Proverbs 3:8 describes the benefits of putting verses 5-7 into practice. Ask the Lord to refresh you with His presence as you wait on His activity.

DAY 3
PRAYER PROMPT

READ ISAIAH 40

After reading Isaiah 40, write out who God reveals Himself to be in this passage. Simply remembering who God is builds our faith. Anticipate fresh revelations about who He is and what He is doing. Notice how He strengthens those who wait for Him in verses 29-31. Tell Him where you are experiencing weakness. Ask Him to renew your strength as you expect Him to act on your behalf.

_____

_____

_____

_____

_____

_____

_____

_____

_____

_____

_____

_____

_____

_____

_____

_____

_____

_____

DAY 4
PRAYER PROMPT

READ ISAIAH 53 AND HEBREWS 4:14-16

I pray you experience incredible comfort as you think about the reality of Him identifying with your grief and sorrow. He understands your disappointment and knows exactly how you feel. Write out all of the ways He suffered for you as described in Isaiah 53.

Reread Hebrews 4:14-16. Consider what it means that Jesus can sympathize with your weakness. Tell Him about the emotions this season of waiting is creating for you—it may help to write them out. You can be gut-level honest with Him. Ask Him to help you respond in an emotionally healthy way. Thank Him for His care, and ask Him to strengthen your trust in Him.

_____

_____

_____

_____

_____

_____

_____

_____

_____

_____

_____

_____

_____

_____

_____

DAY 5
PRAYER PROMPT

READ PSALM 27:13-14, 33:20-22, 40:1-5, AND ISAIAH 30:18

Describe the instruction you find in these passages of Scripture. Clearly, faith *requires* times of waiting. Ask God to increase your faith as you wait. Pray that you, like the psalmist, will be able to say, "My soul waits for the Lord; He is my help. My heart is glad in Him because I trust in His holy name." Write out what it looks like for you to wait on God in this season.

Then consider who is watching you wait on God and pray specifically for them by name. Ask the Lord to show them His faithfulness. And pray to be an example of faith in the waiting so that others can believe.

_____

_____

_____

_____

_____

_____

_____

_____

_____

_____

_____

_____

_____

_____

_____

_____

END-OF-THE-WEEK JOURNAL PROMPTS

1) Which portion of Scripture stood out to you this week and why?

_____

_____

_____

_____

_____

_____

_____

_____

2) Read through the seven insights shared in this lesson from John 11. Which of those seven insights encourages you the most right now?

_____

_____

_____

_____

_____

_____

_____

_____

3) Think about a time when God seemed slow to respond, and describe the emotions you felt while you were waiting.

_____

_____

_____

_____

_____

_____

_____

_____

4) What practices helped you the most while in that time?

_____

_____

_____

_____

_____

_____

_____

_____

5) Write out a verse you've clung to while you were waiting on God to respond.

_____

_____

_____

_____

_____

_____

_____

_____

WRESTLING WITH HIS WILL

WRESTLING

PSALM 22

In the last section we looked at the beautiful, behind-the-scene reality of Jesus intentionally waiting to respond to Martha's and Mary's request to heal their brother. Their time of waiting ended in a miraculous victory! However, this isn't always how God chooses to respond. Many times we pray earnestly, trust Him wholeheartedly, wait expectantly, and He answers differently than we hope He will.

We've all been there. We desperately need something to make sense—we pray, and confusion lingers. Someone we love is diagnosed with cancer—we pray for their healing, and yet they suffer and die. Our child is struggling—we pray, and their battle continues. We desperately need an open door—we pray, and we can't even find a hallway. God asks us to do something difficult—we pray for Him to accomplish His work another way, and we end up with the assignment.

The challenges we face can rattle our faith. When I think back to the most difficult seasons in my own life—the struggle was real! God seemed distant. I found myself questioning God's goodness, wondering if He really loved me, and doubting my ability to hear His voice. These have been some of the most miserable moments in my life. So, what do we do when life is really hard and God doesn't seem to intervene? How do we process the confusion, disappointment, and pain when His response leads us *more deeply into* a difficulty rather than delivering us from it?

Even as followers of Jesus, what we know and what we feel can be in conflict with one another. We read how God's ways are so much different than ours (Isaiah 55:8-9). And we may believe He is working all things together for our good (Romans 8:28). However, simply knowing these truths doesn't remove the challenges of wrestling through really tough questions and doubts. *Just trust and obey* is obviously the right answer, but it doesn't come easily or automatically. With every new challenge we have to work our way through the doubt to a deeper place of trust and obedience to Him.

> Just trust and obey is obviously the right answer, but it doesn't come easily or automatically. With every new challenge we have to work our way through the doubt to a deeper place of trust and obedience to Him.

Have you ever wondered why we have challenges to wrestle through? *Why can't life be easy?* James, the brother of Jesus, gives us some insight. He says, "Consider it pure joy, my brothers and sisters, whenever you face trials of many kinds, because you know that the testing of your faith produces perseverance. Let perseverance finish its work so that you may be mature and complete, not lacking anything," (James 1:2-4, NIV). While our human nature longs for everything to be comfortable, fulfilling, and profitable, Scripture tells us we are refined by the difficulties we encounter. Wrestling is an important part of our spiritual journey, for without it, we don't grow.

In this session, we will look at what Scripture tells us about the idea of wrestling through difficulties with God. The keywords in that sentence are "**with God**." Life's challenges create turmoil in our hearts and minds—what we feel and what we believe become muddied and confused. The enemy of our souls would love for us to pull away from God and try to make sense of things in our own wisdom. If we wrestle apart from God, Satan can feed our doubts, stir up fear, and cause us to pull away from truth, making us vulnerable to lies. His goal is to separate us from all that is good in our lives, but God wants us to press in even closer to His heart and work through these things **with Him**.

We see the idea of wrestling **with God** in several passages of Scripture. In Genesis 32, Jacob wrestled with God to receive His blessing. In Exodus 3-4, we read how Moses wrestled with God over what He was asking him to do. Hannah wrestled **with God** about her desire to have children in 1 Samuel 1. We even read how Jesus wrestled with God's plan in the Garden of Gethsemane (Matthew 26, Mark 14, Luke 22). Each of these individuals wrestled **with God**.

Scripture also shows us individuals who wrestled apart from Him. God asked Jonah to go and share His message of repentance with the people of Nineveh, but Jonah obviously did not want to go. Instead of wrestling with God about this assignment, he fled. "But Jonah rose to flee to Tarshish **from the presence of the LORD**." Later in the same verse, it repeats, "away from the presence of the Lord" (Jonah 1:3, ESV). Rather than wrestling **with God** through his frustration about what He was asking him to do, Jonah ran away and ended up in the belly of a big fish—isolated and miserable.

We will all wrestle with hard times, tough questions, and difficult assignments in life, but *where* we wrestle through the turmoil determines so much. If we turn in to God's presence and wrestle **with Him**, we will be refined by those things and conformed into the image of Jesus. However, if we choose to run away from His presence and wrestle in our own understanding or in the council of unwise people, we will grow bitter and distant from God.

So, what does it look like to wrestle in His presence? In the seasons I've wrestled, the psalms help give voice to my heart. Let's take a look at one of the psalms of David and consider what we learn from his struggle.

READ PSALM 22

For those of us who have read the account of Jesus' death, the first verse of this psalm is familiar to us. They are the same words Jesus spoke on the cross, "My God, my God, why have you forsaken me?" The psalmist continues, "Why are you so far from saving me?" I'm so thankful for this inside look at David's honest struggle. David is described by God as a man after His own heart, and yet we clearly see his frustrations that God isn't responding in the way and time he hopes He will. It's important for us to remember that even though this psalm may only take us a few minutes to read, it might have taken David weeks or months to work through these emotions with God. This psalm doesn't tell us how and when God responded—that too may have taken longer than David hoped. Take some time to read this psalm slowly and consider how the psalmist is engaging **with God**.

#1 Psalm 22:1-2

David is honest with God about his frustration with Him.

#2 Psalm 22:3-5

He intentionally remembers Who God is by considering what He knows from Scripture—how He interacted with His people in the past.

#3 Psalm 22:6-7

David describes how he feels. He even describes how he is being mocked for his trust in the Lord.

#4 Psalm 22:9-10

He recounts who God has been to him personally.

#5 Psalm 22:11

David requests God's presence and help, and acknowledges there is no one else he can trust.

#6 Psalm 22:12-13

He describes his situation to God.

#7 Psalm 22:14-15

David tells God how he feels, and he admits his weakness.

#8 Psalm 16-18

He then tells God *why* He feels the way he does.

#9 Psalm 19-21

He pleads with God for His intervention.

#10 Psalm 22-31

David declares how He will give God the glory when He comes to his rescue. He describes how others will be impacted when they hear how God responds.

David chose to engage honestly **with God** through this hardship. Many of his psalms reflect a similar pattern. It appears that David consistently processed life **with God**—in times of battle, loss, failure, betrayal, and fatigue. Whatever the hardship, David didn't pull away from God. He was gut-level honest with Him. Maybe that is what it means to be a "man after God's own heart." I believe God wants us to stay engaged with Him no matter what is going on in our own hearts and minds.

As we look closely at this psalm and many others like it, we see principles to guide us as we wrestle with God through the hard places in life.

» **Honesty**—Like David, we can admit to ourselves and to God the frustration we feel with His slowness or the disappointment we experience because of the way He responds.

» **Transparency**—This psalm describes the depth of emotion David was experiencing. He doesn't seem to hold anything back. We can be just as transparent with God.

» **Acknowledgement**—Throughout the psalms, even those when David is wrestling through difficulty, he turns his attention off of the situation and on to God. He states what He knows to be true about God from Scripture and how God has revealed Himself to him personally.

» **Humility**—David knew God was the source and proclaims his dependence on Him. Once we acknowledge our inability to make sense of things on our own, we can tell God how much we need His help. This confession opens us to hear clearly from God and receive His insights, blessings, and corrections.

> It appears that David consistently processed life with God—in times of battle, loss, failure, betrayal, and fatigue. Whatever the hardship, David didn't pull away from God.

» **Time**—David took copious amounts of time to pen the psalms. In these prayers, he quotes Scripture and recounts how God has worked on his behalf—revealing the time he spent reading the Law and considering God's goodness and love. We too have to be willing to take the time to dig deep in Scripture. We can allow His Word to shine a light on our thoughts, attitudes, and behaviors. His Word is His side of the "wrestle." We can't wrestle with Him apart from His Word.

» **Obedience**—We have to respond in submission to what the Written Word reveals to us about God and ourselves.

» **Tenacity**—We must be willing to hang in there until our heart is at peace and our faith is renewed.

As a young adult, I didn't know how to navigate the difficulties and tough questions in life *with* God. The lack of openness with God left me open to lies that shaped an incorrect view of God and myself. I'm so thankful for a study on the psalms that started me on a journey of honestly working through my challenges *with* Him. I don't have it all figured out—wrestling with God is messy and looks different for each one of us. However, I know that He wants us to wrestle with Him not apart from Him. And we can engage with Him like David did. I pray these principles help you to process all of your doubts and emotions in His presence.

DAY 1
PRAYER PROMPT

Matthew 19:16-30

We don't know exactly what was going on in the heart and mind of the rich young ruler. However, we clearly see how he walks away when Jesus asks Him to sell his possessions and give to the poor. Rather than simply walking away, he could have engaged with Jesus and tried to understand why He asked this sacrifice of him. He could have asked Jesus to explain what He meant when He said, "you will have treasures in heaven." He could have admitted his difficulty in doing what Jesus asked, and he could have asked for His help. I'm sure Jesus would have responded, for Jesus continues the discussion with His disciples (verses 23-30). Jesus tells them, "With man this is impossible, but with God all things are possible." The young ruler could have discovered what he needed to have eternal life if he had wrestled through his doubt and fear with Jesus rather than walking away.

Is Jesus asking you to give something up? If so, it isn't an arbitrary ask; it is for a reason. Engage with Him, dig deep into Scripture (starting with Matthew 19:23-30), sit in silence and ask Him to speak to your heart. Don't allow the anticipated pain of loss to cause you to walk away. Work through the questions and emotions with Him.

_____

_____

_____

_____

_____

_____

_____

_____

_____

_____

_____

_____

DAY 2
PRAYER PROMPT

READ EXODUS 3-4

When Moses turned aside to see the burning bush, God proceeded to talk with him about the condition of His people who were enslaved in Egypt. God had a big assignment for Moses. We see how Moses isn't thrilled with what God is asked him to do. He had a lot of doubts and questions, but he doesn't walk away from God. He hangs in there and wrestles through the assignment with Him.

Is God asking you to do a difficult thing? The easy thing is to walk away, but the best thing is to humbly tell God how you feel and listen intently for His responses. Reread Exodus 4:10-17 and allow the Lord to speak to your situation from this passage. Be honest with God about the inadequacies you feel and then declare what you know about God. How can you submit to what He is asking you to do today?

_____

_____

_____

_____

_____

_____

_____

_____

_____

_____

_____

_____

_____

DAY 3
PRAYER PROMPT

READ PSALM 73

Psalm 73 clearly describes the difference in wrestling apart from the presence of God and in His presence. The psalmist, Asaph, struggles when he sees how the arrogant prosper. There is a dramatic shift in verse 16. Read verses 16-28 slowly. How does Asaph describe what it was like wrestling apart from God? How did Asaph change after he "went into the sanctuary of God"? I love verse 28, "But for me it is good to near God!" This is the reward, and the wrestle is worth it!

What stands out the most to you from this psalm? Ask the Lord to show you if you have tried to make sense of some injustice apart from His presence. Then consider how you can follow the pattern of this psalm to process your thoughts and keep yourself from becoming embittered.

_____

_____

_____

_____

_____

_____

_____

_____

_____

_____

_____

_____

_____

_____

_____

_____

DAY 4
PRAYER PROMPT

Genesis 32:22-32

Throughout his entire life, Jacob had always depended on himself and his ability to scheme ways to get what he wanted. We know that even his name means "deceiver," a label that proved accurate in his dealings with his brother, Esau. Later we see Jacob being deceived by his uncle, Laban, but then getting his revenge by gaining his uncle's flocks and finally escaping with his family. Now in Genesis 32, his schemes seem ready to catch up with him as a dreaded reunion with his brother approaches.

The night before this dreaded meeting, Jacob wrestles with God. It's quite a scene, but Jacob's entire life, his history of self-sufficiency, is at stake. He is humbled by the threat of Esau's revenge and no scheme seems available to save him now. He is persistent! He fights for God's blessing because he knows there is no other answer. And that's also why the angel asks for his name. In that moment, more than Jacob's hip is wounded. He must acknowledge his deceptive history and in doing so admit that only God can give him the future He promised. Then Jacob gets a new name—Israel, which means prince with God—and a new reputation as one who wrestled with God. In wrestling with God, Jacob understood what it meant to submit to God's plan and die to his flesh.

When we wrestle with God, He is ready to change us too. And when we surrender our short-comings, like Jacob, we prevail as well and experience the future He has for us. Have you come to the end of yourself? Do you need to be as persistent as Jacob in wrestling with God for His blessing? What do you need to admit to God—fear, self-reliance, doubt . . . ?

_____

_____

_____

_____

_____

_____

_____

DAY 5
PRAYER PROMPT

READ MATTHEW 26:36-46, MARK 14:32-42, LUKE 22:39-46

This is such a sacred moment in the earthly life of Christ, and I'm so grateful Matthew, Mark, and Luke include this part of Jesus's journey in their accounts of the Gospel. We can't even begin to understand the pain Jesus was about to endure—the physical pain, yes, but even more the indescribable agony of bearing the sin of the world. Jesus understood fully the outcome and knew He would soon be reunited with His Father in Heaven; however, He still pleaded with God to remove it if there was any way possible.

While we will never be asked to do what Jesus did for us on the cross, we will be asked to walk through pain—the loss of someone we love, a debilitating injury or illness, unfair discrimination or mistreatment . . . But Jesus shows us how to walk the most difficult paths of all. He asks a few of His friends to join Him in prayer, He cries out to God, and He is honest about His desire to not endure what the situation demanded. However, in the end, He trusts His Father enough to say, "Not my will, but yours be done,"?

In light of Jesus's journey, how do you want to respond when God, through the circumstances of your life, asks you to do something you don't want to do? How should you pray? What would it look like for you to surrender to His will in your life right now? How can submitting to His will change you?

_____

_____

_____

_____

_____

_____

_____

_____

_____

_____

END-OF-THE-WEEK JOURNAL PROMPTS

1) Which portion of Scripture stood out to you this week and why?

_____

_____

_____

_____

_____

_____

2) Why is it important to wrestle through doubt, pain, frustration, fear, disappointment, and questions *with* God rather than apart from Him?

_____

_____

_____

_____

_____

_____

3) How would you describe wrestling with God in your life?

_____

_____

_____

_____

_____

_____

4) Consider the persistence of Jacob—do you need to be more persistent in your commitment to live the life God designed for you to live?

_____

_____

_____

_____

_____

_____

5) Describe a time when you wrestled with God. How did it change you? How did it change your understanding of God?

_____

_____

_____

_____

_____

_____

6) Consider the surrender of Jesus. How could your surrender to the will of God change you or the community in which God has placed you?

_____

_____

_____

_____

_____

ANTICIPATING HIS GOODNESS

WEEK EIGHT

ANTICIPATING

NUMBERS 13-14

I have a delightful friend named Lori. I've known her for more than 30 years. And without fail, every time I talk with her, she excitedly tells me what God has done in her life. (And she usually jumps up and down a little, and will enthusiastically clap her hands at some point in the conversation.) God is *always* providing for her in really incredible ways! The girl needs to write a book!

Lori is truly one of the most joyful, authentic, and fruitful people I know. No matter what challenges come her way, Lori honestly anticipates God's faithfulness and goodness to be demonstrated in tangible ways. She rests in the knowledge that God's plans are always the best and she knows there is purpose in His timing. So she doesn't get rattled when things don't come together in an easy, quick way.

The most recent conversation I had with Lori was on a warm, sunny day in Kansas. We were surrounded by food trucks and people eating lunch. True to character, she had some amazing God-intervention moments to tell me. Then she asked me about a situation which happened to be really heavy on my heart. When I finished sharing, she took my hands and prayed the most hope-filled prayer I have heard in a long time. Her response was charged with such expectant faith it almost knocked me off my feet (in a really good way). I walked away from our conversation smiling and anticipating God's activity in a new way. I couldn't help but wonder how her unashamed expectancy must please the heart of God.

Hebrews 11:6 describes God's pleasure in our anticipation this way, "Without faith it is impossible to please him, for whoever would draw near to God must believe that he exists and that he rewards those who seek after him."

My friend Lori is an inspiring example of someone who anticipates God's presence and activity in every part of her life. And she would tell you confidently—while life can be extremely difficult at times, He never disappoints! She experiences such amazing "rewards" as she wholeheartedly believes God will supply every need, each step of the way. (I want to be just like Lori!)

READ NUMBERS 13-14

The Scriptures are filled with examples of individuals who trusted wholeheartedly in God and those who did not. Numbers 13 and 14 describes four men who had great anticipation in God's faithfulness, but they were surrounded by a very large, unbelieving crowd. The contrast in this story helps us to clearly see the importance of anticipating God's activity and how He responds when we anticipate His goodness.

> I couldn't help but wonder how her unashamed expectancy must please the heart of God.

Let's consider what we learn from this part of the Israelites' journey. At this point, the people are free from slavery and are close enough to the Promise Land to send 12 men in to survey the land and bring back a report about what they find.

Before we look at these two chapters, let's think about all these individuals had experienced leading up to this point:

- » God heard their cry for deliverance from slavery. He sent Moses to lead them out of bondage and back to the land promised to their father, Abraham.
- » They witnessed ten horrific plagues which motivated Pharaoh to release them.
- » In the final plague, the death angel passed over their homes, because they obediently sprinkled the blood of a lamb on their doorposts.
- » They received rich plunder from the Egyptians as they were leaving.
- » God parted the Red Sea and allowed them to walk through on dry land.
- » Pharaoh's army was destroyed on the same path when the parted sea closed in on them.
- » They were fed manna from Heaven faithfully every single day.
- » Bitter water was made sweet.
- » The Lord's presence rested on the tabernacle with a cloud by day and a pillar of fire at night. And His presence led them clearly each step of the way.

» Through Moses, they received God's Law and His promises.
» God told them they would take possession of the Promised Land—a land flowing with milk and honey.

#1 Numbers 13:27

When the spies return from surveying the land, they all agreed on one thing—the land is amazing! "It flows with milk and honey," they said. And they showed Moses and people the beautiful produce they found there.

#2 Numbers 13:28-33

Just as soon as the good news is out of their mouths, they turn their focus to the challenges. "The people are strong and the cities are large and fortified" (verse 28). Ten of the men felt certain they would not be able to take the land. However, Joshua and Caleb had a completely different opinion. In fact, Caleb couldn't keep quiet as the other spies spoke of the impossibilities. "But Caleb quieted the people before Moses and said, 'Let us go up at once and occupy it, for we are well able to overcome it'" (verse 30).

#3 Numbers 14:1-4

The people responded with fear and grumbling. They were so afraid, they wanted to choose a new leader and go back to Egypt. That is a lot of fear—somehow brutal slavery seemed better to them than trusting God to bring them into this land victoriously.

#4 Numbers 14:5-9

Moses, Aaron, Caleb, and Joshua knew God was with them and would fulfill His promise to lead them and fight for them. Here is what they said: "The land, which we passed through to spy it out, is an exceedingly good land. If the Lord delights in us, He will bring us into this land and give it to us, a land that flows with milk and honey. Only do not rebel against the Lord. And do not fear the people of the land, for they are bread for us. Their protection is removed from them and the Lord is with us; do not fear them."

Did you notice they equate fear and doubt with rebellion against God? God's response seems to indicate that He saw the unbelief in the same way (verses 11-12).

#5 Numbers 14:10

Instead of trusting God, the people wanted to stone the four leaders who challenged them to believe. (What?!) But the glory of the Lord appeared and stopped them.

#6 Numbers 14:11-12

God is really angry with them, so angry that He considers destroying them and starting over with a new group of people. Moses intercedes for them and God relents His anger and forgives them. But their unbelief cost them dearly—none of them were allowed to enter the land He promised to their ancestors.

The most important thing for us to understand is what made God so angry. He asks, "How long will *they not believe me*, in spite of all the signs that I have done among them?" God simply wanted His children to believe He was able to lead them, fight for them, and provide exactly what they needed. He had already demonstrated His power and provision so clearly! Remember all God had done for them!

#7 Numbers 14:24-37

God honored the faith of Caleb and Joshua. He strengthened them and led them victoriously into the land of promise!

> We face a choice every time we encounter a new difficulty—we can anticipate God's activity and presence, or we can become fearful and grumble.

Our first reaction to the people in this story may be rather critical. How could they doubt God after all they experienced? But then I realized how often we respond like they did. God has done so very much for us! While we didn't witness firsthand the parting of the Red Sea, we can read the account and learn about His power. In fact, we have the entire Bible, filled with His interactions with mankind from the time of Creation through the Apostles' writings. Additionally, we have our own experiences of God's grace and faithfulness to rely on. But we can still find ourselves fearful and grumbling about the challenges we face.

We face a choice every time we encounter a new difficulty—we can anticipate God's activity and presence, or we can become fearful and grumble. Every time I pray, I get to choose whether my heart grumbles its way through, or truly anticipates God's intervention. Let me define those two ideas this way:

» Grumbling happens when our mind is focused on the challenges or on all of things we wish were different in our circumstances.
» Anticipating is the posture of our heart and mind when we trust in the overwhelming goodness of God.

God never promises us ease or prosperity. His promises are so much better than either of those things! He promises He will never leave us or forsake us. He promises that when we seek Him, we will find Him. He promises to give us wisdom and strength. He promises to work all things together for our good. He promises to fulfill His purposes for our life. He promises to meet all of our needs. There is so much to anticipate!

I pray your prayer time this week is filled with anticipating God's presence and activity like never before!

God never promises us ease or prosperity. His promises are so much better than either of those things!

DAY 1
PRAYER PROMPT

READ EXODUS 14:1-11

After reading this passage, ask yourself if you tend to respond more like the people, with grumbling, or like Joshua and Caleb, with anticipation—be honest. Read verse 11 carefully. What do you hear God saying in this verse? Reread the list of all God had done for the Israelites before this time. Describe your thoughts about their disbelief? How do you think God would have responded if they all believed He would lead them and fight for them? Consider making a list of all of the things God has done for you. Admit to Him where you tend to grumble and ask Him to increase your anticipation in His goodness.

_____

_____

_____

_____

_____

_____

_____

_____

_____

_____

_____

_____

_____

_____

_____

_____

_____

_____

DAY 2
PRAYER PROMPT

READ LUKE 1:26-45

Elizabeth's words to Mary reveal the heart of our Father, "And blessed is she who believed that there would be a fulfillment of what was spoken to her from the Lord." This truth isn't simply for Mary; it is for each of us as we believe He will fulfill His promises. Read through all of the promises listed on the last page of this session. Write out those promises that are most meaningful to you right now. Then pray to grow more confident in His goodness.

_____

_____

_____

_____

_____

_____

_____

_____

_____

_____

_____

_____

_____

_____

_____

_____

_____

_____

_____

DAY 3
PRAYER PROMPT

READ PSALM 91

First, read verses 1-13 in this chapter paying close attention to what you learn about God. Write out the characteristics and activities of God described by the psalmist. Which of the things about the Lord encourage you the most right now? Write out what you think it would look like for you to "dwell in the shelter of the Most High? How can you make Him your refuge and fortress? Then read verses 14-16 and notice this is what God says to those who trust in His love. (Those verses make me weep!) How does this chapter encourage you to anticipate God's activity?

_____

_____

_____

_____

_____

_____

_____

_____

_____

_____

_____

_____

_____

_____

_____

_____

_____

_____

DAY 4
PRAYER PROMPT

Read Psalm 34

This is a beautiful passage describing God's activity on behalf of those who seek Him. Read through these verses, and write out what you learn about God and His response to those who cry out to Him. Consider what you need specifically from Him today, and pray with renewed anticipation for Him to step into the situation in a powerful way. Remember, our anticipation is based in our knowledge of Who God is, not simply on what we think is best.

_____

_____

_____

_____

_____

_____

_____

_____

_____

_____

_____

_____

_____

_____

_____

_____

_____

_____

_____

DAY 5
PRAYER PROMPT

READ COLOSSIANS 1:9-14

This is Paul's prayer for the believers in Colossae and it has become my prayer for you. With great anticipation, I pray you will:

» Understand God's will better and better every day
» Gain spiritual wisdom
» Please God in every way
» Bear fruit through your good works
» Grow in your knowledge of God
» Be strengthened by His power
» Have great endurance and patience
» Be full of the joy of the Lord
» Have grateful hearts

You have been rescued from the dominion of darkness and brought into His kingdom. You have been redeemed by Jesus and have experienced forgiveness of sins. He qualifies you to share in the inheritance of the saints—Heaven!

Oh friend, you have so much to anticipate!

How does this prayer encourage you? Describe how are these things the most significant blessings of God?

_____

_____

_____

_____

_____

_____

_____

END-OF-THE-WEEK JOURNAL PROMPTS

1) Which portion of Scripture stood out to you this week and why?

_____

_____

_____

_____

_____

_____

2) What were your first thoughts about the Israelites' responses in Numbers 13-14?

_____

_____

_____

_____

_____

_____

3) Do you think their experiences with God up to this point should have produced a different reaction? Why do you think they allowed fear to overtake their view of God?

_____

_____

_____

_____

_____

_____

4) How did God respond to their unbelief?

_____

_____

_____

_____

_____

_____

5) How did God respond to the faith of Joshua and Caleb?

_____

_____

_____

_____

_____

_____

_____

6) Finally and maybe most importantly, how do you anticipate God will respond to your trust and reliance on Him?

_____

_____

_____

_____

_____

_____

_____

PROMISES

WHAT YOU CAN ANTICIPATE WHEN YOU ENGAGE WITH GOD

When we expect someone to respond one way and they respond differently, we can experience disappointment and frustration. We expect the barista to fulfill our very specific coffee order. We anticipate the doctor to diagnose and treat our symptoms. And when they don't live up to their job descriptions, we want to find a different barista or doctor. At first glance, this might seem quite practical, even smart. However, this consumer mentality can spill over into our closest relationship. We can treat the ones we love with contempt when they don't live up to our expectations.

While this is true in our relationships with one another, it is also true in our relationship with God. So many times, we pray with certain expectations and He responds differently than we hope He will. We can guard our hearts against bitterness and experience all He has for us when we adjust our understanding of Who He is and *how* He promises to respond. What we are anticipating will determine so much. He never promises to answer all of our prayers the way we desire. Actually, faith isn't believing we will get what we want when we pray, faith is trusting that the way He chooses to respond is the best way imaginable.

> Faith isn't believing we will get what we want when we pray, faith is trusting that the way He chooses to respond is the best way imaginable.

We are human and have such a limited understanding of all that is going on around us; however, we can trust He sees the beginning from the end. He is all-powerful, loving, and always has our best interest in mind. While we can't and shouldn't expect Him to fulfill all our wishes, we can expect Him to be good and do what He says He will do.

HERE ARE JUST A FEW OF THE THINGS YOU SHOULD ANTICIPATE WHEN YOU ENGAGE WITH GOD:

» *He loves you* extravagantly and nothing can separate you from His love (1 John 4:7-10 and Romans 8:37-39).

» *He saves you* when you confess with your mouth that Jesus is Lord and believe in your heart that God raised Him from the dead (Romans 10:9-13).

» *He calls you by name* because *He created you* and has *redeemed you* (Isaiah 43:1)

» *He hears you* when you pray (Matthew 6:6).

» *He answers your prayers* (Matthew 7:7-8).

» *He cares for you* (1 Peter 5:7).

» *He is for you* (Psalm 56:9).

» *He is with you always*. Jesus says He will never leave you (Matthew 28:20).

» *He will speak to you* through His Word (Isaiah 55:1-3).

» *He transforms your thoughts, attitudes, and behaviors* as you engage with Him through His Word (Psalm 19, Psalm 119, and Hebrews 4:12)

» *He forgives you* anytime you confess your sins and *removes your sins from yo*u (1 John 1:9 and Psalm 103:12).

» *He provides a way of escape from the temptations* you face (1 Corinthians 10:13).

» *He promises you will find Him* when you seek Him with all of your heart (Jeremiah 29:13-14).

» *He disciplines you for your good* and uses the hard things in your life to *build your character* (Hebrews 12:3-17 and Romans 5:1-5).

» *He will be with you* when you walk through the "fires and the floods" of life and will *not allow you be overcome by them* (Isaiah 43:2).

» *He gives wisdom* when you ask Him for it in faith and don't doubt (James 1:5-6).

» *He brings peace* to your heart when your thoughts are fixed on Him and you trust Him (Isaiah 26:3).

» *He works all things for your good, to conform you into the image of His Son* (Romans 8:28-29).

» *He renews your strength* (Isaiah 40:27-31)

» *He restores your soul* (Psalm 23:2).

» *He offers you rest* (Matthew 11:28-30).

» *He comforts you* (2 Corinthians 1:3-4).

» *He fulfills His purposes for your life* (Psalm 138:8).

» *He teaches you and leads you with His watchful eye upon you* (Psalm 32:8).

» *He will meet all of your needs* (Philippians 4:19).

» **He has good plans for you**—plans for a hope and a future (Jeremiah 29:11).
» **He promises you an eternity with Him**—He is preparing a place for you and will take you to be where He is (John 14:1-3, Revelation 21:1-4).

*These are truly the best gifts of the Father! In them, we find
the abundant life Jesus promises us far more than
any material gift could offer.*

EPILOGUE

Friend, I pray you understand these eight principles for engaging with God on a deeper level than when you started this eight-week journey. I pray He has spoken deep truths to your heart and revealed His provision in life-changing ways.

I encourage you to consistently pull away from the busyness of life by **TURNING** aside and giving God your undivided attention. He longs to engage with you, so prioritize undistracted time in His presence and Word.

It is easy to be focused on what is going on around you. So begin your times of engagement by lifting your eyes off of your current circumstances and on to Him. The best way to do this is by **REMEMBERING** who He is and all He has done for you. He is good and loving and kind! He is all-knowing and all-powerful. And He is so very faithful to you, His child. It is important to recognize how every good thing you enjoy is a gift from Him, take time to express your gratitude for His goodness.

Engage God's Word as His side of the ongoing, two-way conversation. The Holy Spirit has a beautiful way of opening your heart to the ever-unfolding truth of Scripture. You will discover insights you need specifically for the day in front of you as you are faithful to read His Word. So open the Bible and begin **LISTENING** intently for what He wants to say to you. It is such an important part of your life with Him!

May listening to His Word lead you to **RESPONDING** obediently. Your reactions to what God says will shape your thoughts, attitudes, words, and behaviors. Your fruitfulness will become more impactful as your character grows to reflect the qualities of Christ more and more. This is the most transformational element of engaging with Him.

Know God wants you to fully rely on Him, and He expects you to ask for His help and blessing in your life. When you are **ASKING**, you are revealing faith in His power and love. So continue asking, seeking, and knocking. It pleases His heart when you do.

Oh friend, remember that faith *requires* times of **WAITING**! God's timetable is almost always different than yours. Remind yourself that He is always at work for your good. You can trust His love even when you don't understand the delay.

Even when life is extremely challenging and your heart and mind are filled with turmoil, stay engaged with Him! He isn't rattled by your **WRESTLING** with His will—He just wants you to stay engaged with Him through the process.

And finally, it is so important to guard your heart against grumbling, fearfulness, and doubt—this grieves the heart of God. However, nothing pleases Him more than when you pray with your heart and mind fully **ANTICIPATING** His activity in your situation. While His responses might be different than you hoped, He has your best eternal interest in mind. You can always trust His heart—for He is always good.

I pray you grow more and more aware of His goodness and activity in your life! May your character grow to reflect Jesus in ever-increasing ways. And may you experience all He has for you as you continually engage with Him!

—Kerry

GUIDE FOR A DAY ALONE WITH GOD

PRACTICAL IDEAS FOR ENGAGING WITH HIM

It can be intimidating to set aside several hours or an entire day to meet alone with God. This guide is designed to help you get started. It will take some planning to create the time and space for this engagement, but it will be worth the effort—I promise!

BEFORE

» Take care of all of the details necessary for you to have several (4-8) uninterrupted hours—deciding where you will be, making arrangements for child care or other responsibilities, telling others you are not available until a specified time. . . .

» Decide if you should fast both breakfast and lunch. If you decide not to fast, have light meals prepped ahead of time.

» If you plan to have this time in your home and are distracted by things that need to be done, make sure those things are done ahead of time.

DURING

» Only take your Bible, journal, and pen. Avoid using technology. Our devices can be distracting. (Those ads in my Bible app get me every time!) You may want to bring several translations of the Bible if you have them available to you. Reading the verses in different translations can bring greater understanding of the passage.

» If you are struggling to engage in any of the activities or understand Scriptures, ask the Lord to help you.

» View the Scriptures you read as God speaking directly to you, and take your time responding to what He says.
» Feel free to use the pattern laid out in this guide, but allow the Holy Spirit to direct this time. Stay attentive to His presence with minimal outside distractions.
» Be comfortable with silence.
» Make sure to get up and move. This will help to keep you engaged throughout the day.

This guide focuses on the practices and Scriptures we studied in this devotional.

TURNING (10-15 MINUTES)
Read Matthew 6:6 and Mark 6:32-32
» Ask the Lord to help you to turn away from all outside distractions as you "go into your room, shut your door and pray to your Father who is in secret" for the next few hours.
» Thank Him for the opportunity to get away by yourself and engage with Him.
» Consider what Jesus means when He says, "And your Father who sees in secret will reward you."
» Make a commitment to give Him your attention for the next few hours.

REMEMBERING (45 MINUTES TO 1 HOUR)
Read Psalm 145
» After reading this psalm, write out the attributes of God you need to remember most right now.
» Take some time to thank Him for His gifts by writing out all of the good things in your life.
» Remember the major events throughout your life—both the negative and the positive. Then consider how God was actively involved every step of the way.

LISTENING (45 MINUTES TO 1 HOUR)
Read Isaiah 55
» Write out what you believe the Lord has spoken to you throughout the past eight weeks. Is there a reoccurring theme in the Scriptures you've read, sermons you've heard, songs you are drawn to, or conversations you've had?
» What do you hear the Lord whisper in your heart as you quiet yourself in His presence?

TAKE A WALK (15-20 MINUTES)
» Take an outdoor walk, if possible, or do some exercise indoors. As you move, stay attentive to His voice and thank Him for all of the good things in your life.

RESPONDING (45 MINUTES TO 1 HOUR)
Read Psalm 139

» Tell the Lord how you want to respond to those things He has spoken specifically to your heart over the past eight weeks.

» Pray Psalm 139:23-24. Then sit quietly and allow the Holy Spirit to point out if something needs changing in your thought life, attitudes, or responses.

» Respond in repentance and ask God for His help to live in a way that pleases Him.

ASKING (45 MINUTES TO 1 HOUR)
Read Matthew 6-7

» Consider why Jesus tells us to keep on asking, keep on seeking, and keep on knocking. How does He say God responds to those who do?

» Write out those situations that are heavy on your heart today. Express your trust in Him for every situation.

» Think about the week in front of you, tell Him where you need His guidance or help?

TAKE A WALK (15-20 MINUTES)

» Take an outdoor walk, if possible, or do some exercise indoors. Before you start the exercise, read back through Matthew 6-7 and notice the passage of Scripture that stands out to you the most. As you walk, consider those verses in a deeper way.

WAITING (45 MINUTES TO 1 HOUR)
Read Psalm 13

» Consider the situations where you are waiting for God to intervene.

» Acknowledge the emotions and disappointments you are feeling. Remember He is moved with compassion by the sorrow you feel. Ask the Lord to readjust your thoughts and attitudes and build your faith in Him.

» Open your heart to what the Lord wants to teach you as you wait. Write it out in your journal.

WRESTLING (45 MINUTES TO 1 HOUR)
Read Matthew 26:36-46, Mark 14:32-42, Luke 22:39-46

» What stands out to you about Jesus' prayer in the Garden of Gethsemane?

» Is God asking you to do something really difficult? How does Jesus's example in these passages of Scripture encourage you to engage with God?

» Take some time to honestly wrestle through the current struggle you feel.

TAKE A WALK (15-20 MINUTES)

» Take an outdoor walk, if possible, or do some exercise indoors. Stay aware of His presence and enjoy the peace of simply being with Him.

ANTICIPATING (45 MINUTES TO 1 HOUR)
Read Psalm 145:13

» This verse tells us "The Lord is trustworthy in all he promises and faithful in all he does." Read through the list of **"What You Can Anticipate When You Engage With Him"** at the end of session eight.
» Is your faith in getting what you want or in trusting God enough to accept His response as the best response?
» What could God have for you that is even better than what you think you need?

Journal Prompts for the Close of Your Day Alone with God

» What specific things did you hear God speaking to you today?

» Did you sense His encouragement regarding a current challenge?

» Did He reveal any correction about specific thoughts, attitudes, or behaviors?

» Is there anything you want to start doing or need to stop doing?

» Did He give you clear direction for the decision you are facing? What do you need to do?

» How do you feel about your relationship with Him after giving this dedicated time to Him?

» What stands out to you the most as you come to the end of this time alone with God?

» What do you want to remember?

» Should you set up the next time you will meet alone with Him?

SMALL GROUP GUIDES

SMALL GROUP GUIDE—WEEK ONE

1) Use the "End-of-the-Week Journal Prompts" as the discussion questions.
2) Allow each one to share where they most want to make adjustments so they can turn fully towards God and experience all He has for them.
3) Realize as you share your responses, He is with you and hears the desires of your heart. Take time to pray for one another.
4) Encourage one another to recognize the things that are "worth less" than their pursuit of God.

SMALL GROUP GUIDE—WEEK TWO

1) Use the "End-of-the-Week Journal Prompts" as the discussion questions.
2) Ask each one to share one of the good gifts in their life as a way to express their gratitude for His activity in their lives.
3) End the time together by thanking Him for who He is and what He does.
4) Encourage one another to think about His character and His goodness.

SMALL GROUP GUIDE—WEEK THREE

1) Use the "End-of-the-Week Journal Prompts" as the discussion questions.
2) Read aloud Isaiah 55.
3) Pray for God's Word to accomplish what He purposes in each person's life as they listen diligently in the coming week.
4) Encourage one another to "listen diligently" to His Word.

SMALL GROUP GUIDE—WEEK FOUR

1) Use the "End-of-the-Week Journal Prompts" as the discussion questions.
2) Allow each person to share how they want to respond to one thing God spoke to them this week.

3) Pray for one another to respond well.

4) Encourage one another to keep a tender heart of repentance when they engage with God.

SMALL GROUP GUIDE—WEEK FIVE

1) Use the "End-of-the-Week Journal Prompts" as the discussion questions.

2) Give each person the opportunity to share one request they have for the next day—something that is right in front of them. It may be a task at work, a decision that needs to be made tomorrow, wisdom for interacting with a child or a spouse, or a bill that needs to be paid.

3) After the requests have been made, assign everyone one person to pray for specifically. Commit to pray for one another throughout the following day.

4) Encourage everyone to keep asking, seeking, and knocking because our Father gives good things to those who ask Him!

SMALL GROUP GUIDE—WEEK SIX

1) Use the "End-of-the-Week Journal Prompts" as the discussion questions.

2) Pray for those in your group that are in a season of waiting.

3) Promise to pray for one another until you meet again in person.

4) Encourage one another to look for what God wants to speak to them in the seasons of waiting.

SMALL GROUP GUIDE—WEEK SEVEN

1) Use the "End-of-the-Week Journal Prompts" as the discussion questions.

2) Read Psalm 139:23-24.

3) Encourage one another to be aware of the doubts, fears, and questions that surface in their hearts.

4) Ask the Lord to help each one learn what it means to wrestle with God and not to wrestle apart from Him.

5) Encourage one another to have the persistence of Jacob and the surrender of Jesus as they engage with God.

SMALL GROUP GUIDE—WEEK EIGHT

1) Use the "End-of-the-Week Journal Prompts" as the discussion questions.

2) Read through the promises listed at the end of Week 8 and ask each one which promise they need to believe and experience right now.

3) Pray for those who are struggling to believe to grow in their confidence in God's goodness.

4) Encourage one another to anticipate the greater gifts of God more than the material.

Note to the small group facilitators:

Visit our website—clarensaucommunications.com,

for ways to create an engaging atmosphere

in your small groups!

CPSIA information can be obtained
at www.ICGtesting.com
Printed in the USA
BVHW011223050522
635666BV00009BA/10

9 781957 369280